BRIGHT NOTES

GONE WITH THE WIND BY MARGARET MITCHELL

Intelligent Education

Nashville, Tennessee

BRIGHT NOTES: Gone with the Wind
www.BrightNotes.com

No part of this publication may be used or reproduced in any manner whatsoever without written permission, except in the case of brief quotations in critical articles and reviews. For permissions, contact Influence Publishers http://www.influencepublishers.com.

ISBN: 978-1-645423-26-3 (Paperback)
ISBN: 978-1-645423-27-0 (eBook)

Published in accordance with the U.S. Copyright Office Orphan Works and Mass Digitization report of the register of copyrights, June 2015.

Originally published by Monarch Press.
Leila B. Gemme, 1974
2019 Edition published by Influence Publishers.

Interior design by Lapiz Digital Services. Cover Design by Thinkpen Designs.

Printed in the United States of America.

Library of Congress Cataloging-in-Publication Data forthcoming.
Names: Intelligent Education
Title: BRIGHT NOTES: Gone with the Wind
Subject: STU004000 STUDY AIDS / Book Notes

CONTENTS

1) Introduction to Margaret Mitchell — 1

2) Themes and Techniques — 10

3) Textual Analysis
   - Part One: Chapters One Through Seven — 17
   - Part Two: Chapters Eight Though Sixteen — 26
   - Part Three: Chapters Seventeen Through Thirty — 33
   - Part Four: Chapters Thirty-One Through Forty-Seven — 41
   - Part Five: Chapters Forty-Eight Through Sixty-Three — 50

4) Character Analyses — 56

5) Criticism — 93

6) Essay Questions and Answers — 97

7) Bibliography — 103

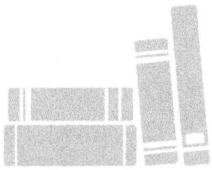

INTRODUCTION TO MARGARET MITCHELL

MISS MITCHELL AND MRS. MARSH

Margaret Mitchell was born in Atlanta, Georgia, in 1900 and lived there all her life. Like her famous leading lady, Scarlett O'Hara, Miss Mitchell's ancestors were planters of cotton in the areas around Atlanta before Atlanta was a city. Her father was Eugene Muse Mitchell, an attorney and President of the Atlanta Historical Society. And her mother, Maybelle Stephens, shared the family's avid interest in local history.

As a child, Margaret Mitchell was steeped in the history of her area. Time and again, she listened to elderly relatives recount the joys of the antebellum period, refight the battles of the war, and relive the ignominies of the Reconstruction. Indeed, Margaret Mitchell had a wealth of source material for a Southern novel in her more distant ancestry. On both sides she was descended from longtime American families and some of her ancestors bear distinct resemblances to characters who appear in *Gone With the Wind*. One in particular, her maternal great grandfather, had a career remarkably similar to Gerald O'Hara's. He escaped from Ireland with the English at his back, eventually settled in Georgia, engaged in trade and ultimately became a planter. He married the daughter of an established, old, Catholic family and took her to live in upcountry Georgia with him, as does Gerald in the novel.

EDUCATION

Margaret was educated at local Atlanta schools and attended the Washington Seminary there from 1914 to 1918. She then went to Smith College in Northampton, Massachusetts, but her college career ended after one year, with the death of her mother. This necessitated her return home to keep house for her father and brother which occupied her until 1922.

During this period Margaret busied herself with the social concerns of a young debutante. She partied, was popular with young men, and saw her future as a young Atlanta matron. Consequently in September of 1922, she married a young North Carolinian named Berrien K. Upshaw. The marriage was destined to last only a few months because Upshaw was emotionally unstable and this instability became clear shortly after the wedding.

CAREER IN JOURNALISM

Within a few months her husband had left Atlanta, and Margaret sought a new life. In December, 1922, she joined the Atlanta Journal. For this paper she wrote regular staff-reporting stories and some features under the by-line Peggy Mitchell. Her writing was very popular locally but really showed none of the promise of what was to come.

Three years later in 1925, Peggy Mitchell married John Marsh, a former copy-reader, and then an executive with the Georgia Power Company. Peggy was an excellent conversationalist and the

Marshes gave many interesting parties in Atlanta in the twenties. She was a tiny woman, with auburn hair and the flawless, milky complexion she attributes to the heroine of her novel. But her energy far surpassed the bounds of her small stature.

WORK ON NOVEL BEGINS

A year after her marriage Margaret Mitchell hurt her ankle so severely that she was forced to leave her job at the *Atlanta Journal*. It was then, in 1926, that she began her momentous novel, most of which was finished in 1929. During this period she suffered many interruptions in her work due to her own poor health and that of members of her family.

Some work continued on the novel but by 1935 only she and her husband had seen the manuscript. It was then that a vice president of the Macmillan Publishing Company came to Atlanta scouting for new American authors. He prevailed upon Margaret Mitchell and eventually got her to show him the book which he knew at once he would publish.

The next eight months Margaret Mitchell spent checking and re-checking historical data in preparation for publication. But no one was prepared for the whirlwind which followed publication in 1936. It was to bring lasting changes to Margaret Mitchell's quiet life.

FAME AND LOSS OF PRIVACY

Gone With the Wind met with such phenomenal popular success that it became a full-time job just to be its author. In the years that followed its publication, Margaret Mitchell spent much of her time answering the tens of thousands of letters the novel provoked. She was also kept busy with interviews, lectures, and book-autographing. Both she and her husband tried valiantly to cling to the life they had known before the book came out. They kept the same apartment and saw the same friends, but *Gone With the Wind* dominated their lives. With the release of the motion picture in 1939, privacy was all but gone.

In these years Margaret Mitchell grew to resent the enormous intrusions upon her life brought about by the success of her novel. Aside from the countless letters and invasions of her privacy was her frequent appearance in gossip columns which printed excessive amounts of misinformation about her. There were unending rumors about her health and the state of her marriage and her relationship with the publishers and whether she actually had written the book or not. Since she had never expected the fame that had come to her, she was unprepared for the onslaught of publicity and never really adjusted to it.

In addition to the amount of work created by being the author of such a successful book, Miss Mitchell's life was complicated, in the years after publication, by her own ill health and that of others close to her. Shortly after publication she was to undergo the terror of having her eyesight fail. Eye hemorrhages, caused by strain and overwork, were to blame. It was several weeks before she could assume a working schedule. In 1943, she underwent a back operation to correct a continuously painful condition resulting from riding accidents as a child and an automobile accident in the mid-1930s.

In addition to her own sickness, she was busied by the illnesses of her father whose condition demanded much attention from 1938 until his death in 1944. And then, in 1945, her husband, John, suffered a massive heart attack. His recovery was very slow and he was never able to return to his job at Georgia Power. When recovered, he concerned himself with much of the business generated by *Gone With the Wind*.

With all of these pressures upon her, Margaret Mitchell never really had time to return to writing although her public clamored for more. Frequently in the years after 1936 rumors would fly that she was working on something new, another novel or perhaps a sequel. She always denied them but they persisted.

DEATH AT 49

On August 11, 1949, Margaret and John were crossing Peachtree Street on their way to the movies when an off-duty taxi driver shot out of control and hit Margaret. She suffered severe head injuries and never regained consciousness, dying on August 16. Her death caused world-wide notice and expressions of regret, much of which centered on the **theme** of her having written only one book.

If she had written more the world would never have known because, under the terms of her will, all her papers were destroyed. The only exception was enough of the original manuscript of *Gone With the Wind* to prove her authorship should that ever be necessary. But that seems highly unlikely. Margaret Mitchell brought to her task such a unique combination of background and talent that there could be little doubt that she herself had produced this magnificent work.

WRITING AND PUBLISHING "GONE WITH THE WIND"

After Margaret Mitchell resigned from the Atlanta Journal, in ill health because of her improperly healed ankle, she read deeply into the background of her locality. A natural writer, she was always inventing stories, devising plots, and building characters. So when she sat at the typewriter in 1926 to begin her long work, she had it outlined in her mind in total. In fact, she wrote the end first and worked backward through the book, chapter by chapter.

As chapters were completed, she stored them in envelopes which began to accumulate in the Marsh's small apartment. Her work was by no means regular since there were many calls on her time due to illness. Also, research had to be carried out as the book was being written since historical detail plays such an important role in the work. She had to delve deeply into the economic and social aspects of the war and Reconstruction as well as the political history of those times.

Margaret Mitchell wrote directly on the typewriter as do many trained in journalism and much of her revision was done in her own hand, written in between the typed lines. She wrote suggestions for future revisions on the outside of the envelopes. Some plot lines were either incomplete or had more than one possible outcome. And even when submitted, the book had no opening chapter.

Since the outline for the novel was complete in her mind when she began *Gone With the Wind*, she could work on whatever chapter she chose without regard to sequence in the book. Throughout the period of the writing (which was done largely between 1926 and 1929), Miss Mitchell never publicly expressed any real hopes for publication. In fact, she often said she only worked on it to keep herself busy because she had nothing better to do with her time.

SEARCH FOR HEROINE'S NAME

As the novel was originally written, the heroine's name was Pansy O'Hara but neither she nor the publisher was completely happy with it. Margaret Mitchell kept at the problem of the name - Storm O'Hara was considered for a while - until finally during the period of preparation for publication she came up with Scarlett. It was a stroke of genius - she had created what is easily one of the most apt and memorable names in American fiction.

Another problem with names that the author struggled with during the pre-publication period was to ensure that no real names of Atlantans were used. Margaret spent many hours going over old records to check for a duplication of names. The name of the book itself was also a problem. Originally the novel was titled *Tomorrow is Another Day*. This was rejected when it was discovered that the word "tomorrow" was enormously popular in book titles of that time. This was the period of the Depression, and a hopeful "tomorrow" on a book cover was very popular. The search proceeded until Margaret came across Ernest Dowson's poem "Non Sum Qualis Eram Bonae Sub Regno Cynarae," which contains the lines, "I have forgot much Cynara! gone with the wind …" Margaret knew then that she had the proper title for her novel and, indeed, its perfection may have contributed much to the success of the novel.

BUILD-UP AND DENIAL

Miss Mitchell did some work on the novel in the early thirties but seemed to have no intention of pursuing publication. Then, in

1935, Harold Latham of the Macmillan Company began his book-scouting tour in Atlanta. Friends from Margaret's newspaper days had referred him to her and he met Margaret early in his visit at a literary luncheon. She denied that she was working on anything or that she had a manuscript. As his visit to Atlanta lengthened into a few days, Harold Latham discovered more and more people recommending that he see Peggy Mitchell. He was puzzled by the verbal build-up in the face of the author's denial. When he again saw Margaret Mitchell, he pursued the matter but she continued her denials. He did get her to promise that if she ever had anything for publication she would show it to him first. Just before his departure for New Orleans, Mr. Latham received a telephone call from Miss Mitchell asking to see him in the hotel lobby. There he found her with the bulkiest manuscript he had ever seen. She urged him to take it in a hurry before she changed her mind about showing it to him. It was so enormous that it would not fit into any of his luggage and he had to buy a suitcase which is filled completely.

BEST-SELLER FOR TWO YEARS

Harold Latham knew upon first perusal that he had come upon something of vast importance in the publishing world. Contracts were hastily drawn and arrangements with the author concluded. There then began eight long months of preparation for publication during which names were checked and changed, historical data verified, and the novel was titled. Macmillan knew it was on to something very important but no one could have foreseen the deluge that began on publication day - June 30, 1936. The book was selected for the July Book-of-the-Month Club and was to be number one on the nation-wide best seller list for two years. In spite of the Depression, the book sold at its record-breaking three-dollar price. Its enormous success was the financial salvation of hundreds of bookstores during the Depression. Ultimately it was published in twenty-six languages and it was to command the highest motion-picture price ever paid (up to that time) for a first novel.

There were several legal results of publication. One which occurred after Margaret Mitchell's death was the enactment in 1952 of new tax legislation to provide for persons - like the author - who collect in one-year income resulting from many years of work. The need for an income-averaging scheme was dramatized by the enormous taxes Margaret Mitchell had had to pay in 1936 and 1937. Another law effective in 1937 protected prices after price-wars had reduced the earning power of the book.

In 1939 David Selznick released the motion picture version of the story starring Clark Gable and Vivien Leigh as Rhett and Scarlett. Like the book, it enjoyed unheard-of popular success and has had successful re-releases since that time.

GONE WITH THE WIND

THEMES AND TECHNIQUES

THEME

As Margaret Mitchell herself has pointed out, the major **theme** of *Gone With the Wind* is survival. She has set her characters against the background and action of the Civil War and Reconstruction in the South, allowing them to struggle against the currents of history tugging and pulling at them. She wanted to show how it is that some people manage to survive great disasters while others are swept away by them. And in her book the major characters are all tested deeply by the strife that they face.

The kernel thought of her novel was told to Margaret Mitchell when she was a little girl. She had been refusing to go to school and her mother took her out riding on the road that leads South from Atlanta. There they saw many of the old Civil War homes, some in disrepair, some beautifully kept up. Margaret's mother talked of the upheaval that the owners of those homes had faced and that some had succeeded and some failed. She pointed out that when upheavals come everybody becomes equal and all anyone can depend on is his physical strength and the knowledge in his head. Since women's physical strength wasn't worth much, she urged Margaret to go to school, to learn, to protect herself against the day when she might need her knowledge to survive. Rhett Butler echoes the words of Margaret's mother in a conversation he has with Scarlett and, indeed, the **theme** is repeated often in the novel.

Mostly, however, it is exemplified by the major characters and their responses to the action of the novel. Rhett is obviously a survivor, almost happily riding the crest of everyone else's failures. But Rhett has survived the disaster of social ostracism before the war and has made his way in the world successfully without the advantages of social acceptance and his family's money. He will not only survive but will enjoy doing it under these circumstances.

The question of Scarlett's survival provides the major interest of the work. She faces enormous odds, with little preparation for them, creating some of the novel's tension. When her survival becomes clear, the next question is what will survival cost her in terms of her own self-image and the values of her life?

Ashley, it is clear from the beginning, cannot survive such an upheaval of his life as the Civil War. He hasn't the fiber to adjust to the changed circumstances. But the author allows tension to build around the question of when Scarlett will recognize this.

Melanie's survival is more puzzling. Without a great deal of help from others, she would not survive in a material way. Yet her ability to keep her old beliefs and morals intact in the face of such a disaster is a kind of survival in itself.

THE USES OF HISTORY

This **theme** of survival is played out against a piece of history that has provided the American story with its most romantic and exciting moments. The setting is Atlanta, Georgia, during and after the Civil War, and Margaret Mitchell has poured into it the accumulated knowledge of a childhood spent listening to reminiscences of that time. Her own background was a perfect starting place to begin work on such a story because she had acquired so much personal knowledge of her subject by the time she was ready to write her book.

If *Gone with the Wind* is an historical novel, it is, in the main, a novel of social history and it is in this realm that Margaret Mitchell shines. From her mother and other female relatives she had acquired a vast fund of information about the social customs of the period and she incorporates them beautifully into her work. The entire first section shows Scarlett alternately employing and chafing against the social rules which govern her behavior. The whole unnatural set of rules governing relationships between men and women could be manipulated to advantage and, at sixteen, Scarlett was expert at it.

Scarlett's constant breaking of these rules and discovery that nothing horrible results creates interest in the first part of the book. This is especially true after she is widowed and begins to transgress the strictest of all social regulations; those involving the proper behavior of widows. The lessons she learns in doing this will stand her in good stead when the desperate circumstances of war-induced poverty force her to break far more serious rules.

The setting also provides ample opportunity for Miss Mitchell to show how war and disaster contribute to mitigate the stringency of social regulations. The freedom of Atlanta's young ladies to see whom they wanted, to do without chaperones, to marry relative strangers increased in direct proportion to the devastation of the war.

While Margaret Mitchell never describes the fighting directly, she exposes important events to the reader through the reaction of her characters. The siege of Atlanta, for example, is explained not in terms of the battles as they were fought but rather in terms of Atlantans in the city hearing the devastating news and reacting to it. The reader never sees Sherman's men sweeping a sixty-mile-wide path through Georgia but he feels their presence when a small band of them stops to loot Tara. It is through this kind of presentation that the history in the novel remains alive and vital.

NARRATIVE TECHNIQUE

Miss Mitchell's skill in narrative techniques provides a pace that keeps an enormously long novel from waning. The story is told in episodic form with occasional uses of flashback to provide background for a character. These reviews of the past are near the beginning of the book and bring the reader up to date on the backgrounds of characters like Gerald O'Hara, Scarlett's father.

The author provides an interesting alternation between scenic and panoramic narration which adds to the interest of the novel. A good example of this occurs when Scarlett arrives in Atlanta after the birth of her first child. After a panoramic view of the history of the town, Miss Mitchell allows the reader to see it as Scarlett does, detail by detail, as it must have looked that day in 1862, right down to a glimpse of the local "bad woman." The same technique is employed in the last two sections of the book to give an overview of the politics of the Reconstruction period followed by a particular instance of what it was really like. It is an informative and interesting approach and certainly contributes to the perfect timing and pace of *Gone With the Wind*.

CHARACTERIZATION

It is in the area of characterization that this author's work shines most brightly. For she has created characters whose names have become truly "household words" and whose likeness to reality is almost breathtaking.

There are several techniques which the author uses to bring her characters to life. One is that she gives complete physical descriptions of them so that, even without the aid of the motion picture, the reader can create a picture in his mind. In addition, the author leaves the reader with a sense that many characters - even major ones - are not fully exposed. They appear to have sides we cannot see or to think things we do not know about. This is highly realistic because it is true of all human relationships. No one ever knows all about another person. Everyone has his secrets from the world and the characters in *Gone With the Wind* are like real people in this respect.

Another feature which contributes to the reality of Margaret Mitchell's characterization is the fullness of some of her characters. One does not play the role of villain to another's hero. Instead they are all given a share of virtue and some of treachery. The least likely character to choose to exemplify this is Melanie Wilkes, Ashley's almost perfect wife and Scarlett's sister-in-law. Outwardly Melanie appears to be too sweet and good and perfect to be imaginable. But she is neither spineless nor sugar coated. Melanie can be very harsh when she confronts a wrong or something that will hurt her loved ones. Her comment on the Atlanta Home Guard who were assiduously avoiding combat duty by "protecting the home front" is a good example: upon hearing how nice they looked, she remarked that they would look much better "in grey uniforms and in Virginia."

Later, after the war, Melanie, still a real paragon of goodness, exhibits her most damning trait. She is implacably unforgiving of the former foe. While, at the time, it appears as staunch and holy loyalty, in reality, it is the kind of bitter hatred that will not let the wounds of war heal. It is not difficult to suspect that Margaret Mitchell felt a little of this herself.

The most telling test of Miss Mitchell's characters is that they are able to live on in the reader's imagination when he has finished the book. It is possible to imagine them doing things the author did not write off. And, after immersion in the book for a time, reality seems to fade in comparison to the reality of the people in the novel. Few authors can achieve this kind of verisimilitude in their works and those who do are usually very successful.

The best example of the fact that Margaret Mitchell's characters seem to take on lives of their own is the tremendous ado that took place over the question of whether or not Scarlett won Rhett back. It was a topic of social conversation for years after publication. Fights broke out over it. The author received thousands of letters begging for the answer (she always said she didn't know). Many people offered to write sequels and epilogues to answer the unanswered question and, to this day, it haunts first-time readers.

ATTITUDE AND POINT OF VIEW

One of the reasons that Margaret Mitchell always said she was hesitant about showing the manuscript to a publisher was that it had a Southern point of view. She feared rejection by Northern publishers because of this. While her fears were unwarranted, her concept of the point of view is precise. *Gone With the Wind* idealizes the antebellum South with such a lack of criticism that it might be describing another world. Unlike John Brown's Body in which Benet, while describing the luxuriant beauty of aristocratic life, recognizes the ugly injustice of the slave system upon which it is built, *Gone With the Wind* makes no such admission. Only once in the whole long novel is there even a hint of the moral question of slaveholding. That occurs when Ashley says that he would have freed his slaves if the war had not done so first. But, at the same time, he defends slave-holding as less brutal than the convict leasing which went on in Atlanta after the war.

To the modern reader, the racial attitudes expressed in *Gone With the Wind* are almost unbelievable. Miss Mitchell is giving what appears to be an accurate accounting of the attitudes of the times and, from this, it is easier to understand why racial misunderstandings prevail to this day. The white people in the novel look upon the black people in the same light as they see children or beloved pets. It is a socially ingrained attitude, and perhaps the worst social flaw of the novel is that this social attitude is allowed to go uncriticized. In any event, the sources of race difference in America can become abundantly clear after reading such a work.

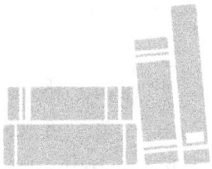

GONE WITH THE WIND

TEXTUAL ANALYSIS

PART ONE: CHAPTERS ONE THROUGH SEVEN

"CHORD OF RECOGNITION"

Part One of *Gone With the Wind* serves largely to introduce the characters of the novel and set up the major tensions therein. It is dominated, not surprisingly, by Scarlett O'Hara, the belle of Tara, and the central figure of the work. Scarlett must be among the most "living" characters in American fiction. She is drawn so realistically, with her baser motivations pitted against the stern **conventions** she must follow, that she strikes an immediate chord of recognition in most readers.

In the third chapter, the author suspends the action to introduce in depth Scarlett's parents, Gerald and Ellen O'Hara. They are important keys to an understanding of Scarlett. Gerald, coming to America to escape English authorities in Ireland, had attained wealth and position through determination and great self-confidence. He had acquired both his valet, Pork, and his plantation, Tara, at the poker table after a good deal of whiskey. At age forty-three, he decided to go courting and against all odds he won the hand of the well-born, beautiful, fifteen-year-old Ellen Robillard of Savannah. Ellen, unbeknownst to Gerald, accepted his proposal to escape Savannah. Her parents had sent away her lover, a distant cousin (Philippe Robillard), and he had been killed. Broken-hearted, she accepted Gerald's proposal and they moved to Tara in north Georgia. Ellen is a very great lady and Scarlett is a product of both of them. Underneath, she is all Gerald: hot-tempered, willful, determined, selfish. On the surface, she is a demure, sweet, Southern belle. But the veneer is thin and there is a good deal of **foreshadowing** that it will crack often.

The author also suspends the action in the introduction of Ashley Wilkes. In chapter two Scarlett mentally reviews her love for the dashing young scion of Twelve Oaks. His return after a three-year European Tour was the occasion of love at first sight for Scarlett and it is possible to see immediately that what she loves about Ashley is that she can't understand him. The other boys and beaux in her life are somewhat simple and transparent but Ashley's intellectuality and variety of interests mystify Scarlett. She is mostly bored by what interests him but the fact that he has a multitude of interests is a compelling factor in her love for him.

SCARLETT'S MOTIVATION

This love of Scarlett's is a motivating force throughout the novel. It determines her course of action in the entire first part of the book and it appears likely to continue to do so. There is an interesting ambivalence in the author's point of view of a match between Scarlett and Ashley. In chapter two, when

Scarlett awaits her father's return home from Twelve Oaks after the Wilkes break the news, Gerald is very much against such a match. Because of their intellectuality or "queerness" as Gerald calls it, the Wilkes have always married distant family who all understand each other. Gerald thinks this is fine: "Like must marry like or there'll be no happiness."

On the other hand, in chapter five, when the O'Hara girls are en route to the barbecue with their father riding alongside and they encounter the four Tarleton girls and their mother, Beatrice, she expresses a different opinion. Beatrice Tarleton is a horsewoman and very interested in breeding. The inbreeding of the Wilkeses, she feels, is leading them to trouble and is responsible for the pale, stringy looks of the Wilkes girls in this generation. Far better, Beatrice thinks, for Ashley to marry one of her four girls or one of the O'Haras and add some new blood to the line.

So, utilizing two different characters, the author outlines pros and cons of a Scarlett-Ashley match. But an incident at the barbecue is the most revealing in terms of what would be wrong in such a match. Rhett Butler informs the gathering that he is of the opinion that the South doesn't stand a chance if war breaks out. It is a shocking and devilish thing to say at a party of such partisans and the crowd seethes. When they quite, Ashley walks to where his cousin Charles Hamilton, who has fallen in love with Scarlett, is seated beside her. "He looks like one of the Borgias," Ashley comments to Charles about Butler. "I don't know them. Is he kin to them?" Scarlett asks. Charles is dumbfounded and embarrassed at this untutored remark from his love. And Ashley looks on Charles with a mixture of understanding and pity.

It is a small moment, but an important one. The author has shown why Scarlett and Ashley (or Scarlett and Charles for that matter) would be unfulfilling to each other and at the same time, given the hint that a passion for Scarlett exists in Ashley. The reader is not sure that the passion is there at present but there is some evidence in Ashley's understanding of Charles' predicament.

RHETT'S UNIQUE ROLE

Rhett Butler's continued importance in the story is indicated by his unique role in Part One. Not only is he the provocateur nearly ruining the barbecue with his ill-omened pronouncements about the South, but also he is the only witness to Scarlett's worst moment: when she is throwing herself at Ashley. He takes the occasion to point out that he and Scarlett are not so very different, a horrifying statement since he is not "received" by the gentry of Charleston because of his ill behavior there.

The barbecue itself takes place three days after the firing on Fort Sumter and the news of Lincoln's call for volunteers breaks up the party even before the ball can begin. This, like Scarlett's love, is another of the major mainstays of the story. For essentially, it is a story of survival in wartime and of the reconstruction that follows. Thus the actual events of history will be closely interwoven with the lives of the characters.

MITCHELL AS SOCIAL HISTORIAN

More than political or military history, however, *Gone With the Wind* is a novel of social history. It depicts in breathtaking, sympathetic detail the glowing aristocracy that was the Old South. Margaret Mitchell, herself a child of the South, writes of the old era lovingly and with enough attention to historical detail to expose a good deal of it to the reader.

These early chapters elucidate in detail the finely drawn social structure that characterized this era. In chapter one, when the Tarleton twins ride away from Tara disappointed at the absence of a dinner invitation, they try to decide where to go to avoid their mother's wrath at their latest expulsion from college. In this conversation with their slave, Jeems, the stratification of Southern society is clear. Jeems, one of a hundred slaves on the Tarleton plantation, looks down on Able Wynder as poor white because Able owns only four slaves. Jeems feels secure because he belongs to such a large, wealthy plantation. Stuart and Brent Tarleton hotly defend Able, acknowledging that he is poor but denying that he is "trash". That epithet they reserve for the Slatterys, a poverty-stricken family, non-slave owners, whose brood increases each year, and who live essentially by begging from the neighbors.

Among the slave population a rigid social structure was maintained. House slaves (with the Mammy at the top) were considered superior to those who worked outside the house. Outside, skilled laborers, such as cobblers or carpenters, were ranked above those who looked after animals and the lowest of all, the field hands. In addition, ownership by a large plantation carried more status than ownership by a small farm.

Throughout chapters two and three these relationships are depicted, setting the social context of the novel. In chapter three, the author points out that the first position a male slave had at Tara was to shoot birds out of the front yard. After this, they were sent to the various plantation tradesmen - carpenter, wheelwright and the like - to learn a skill. If they failed at these tasks they became field hands.

Mammy's position and opinions also help define these social relationships. She frequently belittles other slaves and obviously considers herself above them.

NOVEL OF UPPER-CLASS LIFE

The white social structure is headed by the planter class which is the main focus of the novel. Miss Mitchell gives her readers an occasional glimpse of white trash (like the Slatterys) but largely it is a novel of the upper class. Among the planter class there was a rigid social code that is magnificently exposed in Part One, and, indeed, throughout the novel. Masculine and feminine behaviors are clearly formulated by this code. It is important for men in this social setting to be adept at playing poker, skilled at riding and breeding horses, steady at drinking whiskey, straight at shooting and unfailingly courteous to ladies. Gerald O'Hara possesses all of these talents and the reader is exposed to this entire aspect of the society in the author's description of the master of Tara. It is not necessary for a gentleman planter to have much else in the way of acquired culture. This is evident in Chapter Two when Scarlett and her father discuss the Wilkeses. Their love of the great books, music, and art seems queer to Gerald and he says so. Scarlett defends Ashley by pointing out that he can ride, play poker, and drink as well as any young man in the County. Ashley has mastered all of the techniques of masculinity and, beyond that, the degree of his culture really matters little except for making people believe he is somewhat strange.

SOCIAL CODE FOR PLANTERS' SONS

The description of the Tarleton brothers in chapter one throws further light on the social code of the Old South as it pertained to planters' sons. A great deal of leeway was given them in matters of behavior among themselves. Non-professional gambling, frequent drunkenness, and playful shootouts were tolerated as boyish pranks. A lack of book learning is no stigma at all. After all, the Tarletons have been expelled from four universities and see no shame in it. Only with ladies is their behavior seriously proscribed. Here they must act according to a rigid set of rules governing such things as when in a relationship one is allowed to call a lady by her first name, and what gifts are proper to give her. It is for the breach of this social code that Rhett Butler is not received in Charleston society. In a bit of whispered gossip with Cathleen Calvert, Scarlett learns of Rhett's disgrace. He was out buggy riding with a Charleston girl when the horse ran off and they were unable to return for hours. The gentlemanly thing to do would be to offer to marry the girl that very day, but Rhett refused. The girl's brother challenged him to a duel in which - as Rhett points out later in the book - the gentlemanly thing to do is to get killed. He did not, but killed the brother instead, and thus was not "received" in the nice homes of Charleston.

SOCIAL CODE FOR DAUGHTERS

For girls the code of conduct is extremely rigid. They are to eat little in public, act as if they had no intellect whatsoever, and be continually impressed by the superior ability of the male. With such a structure it was easy to control behavior and reactions and Scarlett mastered it beautifully. She had most of the County boys in love with her by just a few calculated moves in their direction. A good example of this occurs in chapter six when Scarlett first encounters Charles Hamilton at the barbecue. With a few well-chosen words she has him as her willing slave. But Scarlett treads on thin ice. She is so forward that she puts herself in danger of being "fast" and risks being talked about by

County matrons. Certainly this is the case in her conversation with Ashley in the library at Twelve Oaks. Throwing herself at him in such a manner was unheard of and broke every social **convention**. That is why Rhett's eavesdropping caused Scarlett such embarrassment. He had caught her in a situation which proved she was no lady and probably never would be.

SOCIAL CODE FOR WIVES

Life as a matron in this society placed many demands on a woman. For although men may desire empty-headed, simpering, dependent girls, in wives it was something else. Married women were expected to take over the running of the household at a time when households were enormous. And all of the work is done with total deference to the male - to make it seem as if really the women were doing next to nothing. Margaret Mitchell brings out this facet of society best in Ellen O'Hara. A young girl of fifteen when she first comes to Tara as Gerald's bride, she is, none the less, prepared to run the place. It is she who keeps things in constant readiness for visitors, who oversees the working of the slaves, who keeps the accounts of the plantation. Her devotion is made clear on the day of the barbecue when she must stay at home to deal with the matter of Jonas Wilkerson. On the night before the barbecue Ellen is called away at dinnertime to baptize the dying infant of Emmy Slattery. Finding that Jonas Wilkerson, Tara's Yankee overseer, is the father of Emmy's illegitimate offspring, Ellen returns and tells Gerald that he must fire Jonas. This is done on the following morning and it means that someone must remain at home to go over accounts with Wilkerson. Naturally, it is Ellen. Not only does she not complain, but no one gives a thought to the fact that she might like to be at the barbecue or might resent missing the fun. The very idea that Gerald stay at home to handle this matter seems absurd in this society. Planters pursue their pleasurable courses while their wives see that work gets done behind the scenes. It is simply the scheme of things.

NO HINT OF SOCIAL INIQUITY

Gone With the Wind is, then, inimitable social history. The characters which people its pages live out their lives within a certain social structure which the author knows intimately and portrays beautifully. She paints it sympathetically and in detail. Margaret Mitchell has been called an "unreconstructed Southerner", and, indeed, that feeling persists in Part One of her novel. There is no hint here of the evil of a slave system, of the inequities of aristocracy, or of the injustice of a society based on the belief in racial superiority. In fact, there is practically a tacit defense of these things. The only feature of society which seems to receive even a slight critical purview from the author is the treatment of women. Her portrait of Ellen and her lot in life is one of sympathetic understanding. And she comments quite freely in agreeing with Scarlett's displeasure at the poses she must adopt to attract men:

> There was no one to tell Scarlett that her own personality… was more attractive than any masquerade she might adopt. Had she been told she would have been unbelieving. And the civilization of which she was a part would have been unbelieving too for at no time, before or since, had so low a premium been placed on feminine naturalness.

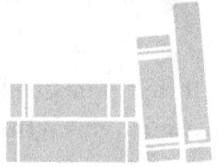

GONE WITH THE WIND

TEXTUAL ANALYSIS

PART TWO: CHAPTERS EIGHT THOUGH SIXTEEN

WOMEN AT WAR

The second part of *Gone With the Wind* gives a clear picture of behind-the-lines life during wartime. Early in this section, the author describes Atlanta in detail. It is a young city, raw and crude (aptly, it is compared to Scarlett), unlike the staid and sleepy Charleston and Savannah. Also it is a town bustling with the business of war. It has grown enormously since the war began: new factories are everywhere and the open spaces are rapidly filling up. Soldiers abound, the different uniforms brightening the streets with color. Many new tasks fall to the women in this war and major among them is nursing. For the young unmarried girls his generally means cheering up convalescent young men, and rolling bandages. For married women and widows, however, it is much less pleasant: they must assist at ghastly operations and tend the dying. And they serve on more than one hospital committee. Scarlett abhors all of it. Margaret Mitchell's Atlanta is peopled by a variety of humans. The rigid old matrons are there in the form of Mrs. Merriwether, Mrs. Elsing, Mrs. Whiting, and Mrs. Meade. In no time they are bearing down on Scarlett for her forward ways. And the town has "bad women", the most notorious of whom is Belle Watling whose dyed red hair amazes all who see it. Scarlett sees Belle on her arrival in Atlanta and can barely believe her eyes.

In chapter eight the author again uses the technique of suspending the action to review the short history of Atlanta. It is such a young town and it has grown so fast that this description foreshadows the excitement to be found there. Here it will surely be possible for Scarlett to shake off the depression that has gripped her and gain some sort of new hold on her life.

CHARACTERIZATION

Certain characters are painted more fully in Part Two and Aunt Pittypat Hamilton is one of these. While she is never a completely delineated individual and remains a type throughout the novel, the reader does become somewhat acquainted with her here. Her real name is Sarah Jane Hamilton but the sound of her tiny feet earned her silly nickname and her adult flutterings keep it relevant. Aunt Pitty has led a sheltered spinster life. She is estranged from her realistic brother, Uncle Henry, and under the thumb of the autocratic old Peter, the slave who really makes things run in the Hamilton household. When Melanie and Charles were orphaned at an early age, Miss Pitty was charged with their upbringing but it was Peter who really made the decisions about their lives. Scarlett finds that she and Melanie must spend a good deal of their time shielding Pittypat from ugly truths and ministering to her fainting spells. Miss Mitchell makes use of Aunt Pittypat as a type character whose demands can be utilized to further the plot line or whose idiosyncrasies are valuable for comic relief.

But it is Melanie who really comes to life in these pages. Several times Rhett Butler refers to her as a truly "great lady" and it is not difficult to see why. She is somewhat similar to Scarlett's mother in certain respects but while Ellen O'Hara remains undelineated, Melanie becomes a real individual. She is a thoroughly good person and she consistently sees the good in others. Melanie desires happiness for everyone and she always manages to see some good or redeeming quality in another to bring about this state of happiness. Scarlett can sneak around and read Ashley's letters and secretly love Ashley and Melanie sees none of it. She only sees what she herself would have been under the circumstances: a bereaved and desolate young widow, sensitive even to the mention of her beloved's name. Since Scarlett can barely remember what Charles looked like, it often happens that Melanie misconstrues Scarlett's motives. When Scarlett cries at missing all the parties and fun, Melanie assumes she's missing Charles and comforts her. This frustrates Scarlett all the more.

Melanie's good-heartedness is best revealed in a scene involving Belle Watling. Belle wants to make a monetary contribution to the Glorious Cause and approaches a worthy Atlanta matron who refuses the money and runs away. When she comes to Melanie, however, her money is accepted with thanks. It is simply outside the bounds of Melanie's character to be cruel to anyone. Unfortunately, Belle wrapped the money in one of Rhett Butler's initialed handkerchiefs, so Scarlett discovers his relationship with the local "fancy house". Her heated, angry reaction to this discovery is ample evidence that she cares more about Rhett than even she herself realizes.

CHANGING VALUES IN WAR-TIME

As for Scarlett, Part Two shows the underside of her character more seriously breaking through the veneer that Ellen and

Mammy had struggled so long to achieve. Scarlett's development in this section of the novel is a perfect vehicle for the social history it reveals. As it opens, Scarlett is a new and young widow in the Old South. Widowhood is the most constrained of all social situations in this society. Rhett Butler likens it to an Indian suttee only instead of throwing herself on her husband's funeral pyre, the Southern widow is buried alive. A widow has no social life at all, certainly none involving men. She is never allowed to laugh and even smiling must be sweet and sad. Her clothing is black from head to toe including a knee-length black crepe veil which could be shortened to shoulder-length after three years of widowhood. Two occurrences aided Scarlett in circumventing these **conventions** of widowhood. One was the Civil War and the other was the arrival of Rhett Butler on the scene. Only as drastic a tool of social change as a war would have allowed Scarlett to attend the bazaar that was the beginning of her emergence from the constraints of widowhood. After this event and her scandalous behavior (which consisted of dancing), Scarlett felt herself relatively free to party and dance and flirt again. Melanie, again seeing the good, defends Scarlett in this. And Melanie's excuse for Scarlett's behavior is that it is wartime and that the three of them have no business shutting themselves up in mourning when so many of the convalescent soldiers need places to visit. The war has brought a good deal of social informality to Atlanta. Families are allowing their daughters to see men they hardly know because the men are available and there is no time to inquire about their families. Melanie's defense of Scarlett and the loosened strictures of wartime behavior are all that keep Scarlett socially acceptable. She gets herself talked about a good deal but she is not ostracized.

Rhett As Catalyst. Rhett Butler is really the catalyst for this breakthrough of Scarlett's. While the combination of the times and Scarlett's own personality might have allowed it to happen, in due time, the author puts Rhett there to encourage it every step of the way. He gets her to dance at the bazaar. He has her admit that she is bored by the noble "Cause" and has little loyalty to it. And ultimately, he contrives to have her give up mourning clothes. For this last he appeals to her vanity by bringing her a hat that matches the green of her eyes. It is stunning on her but Rhett will not allow her to keep it if she covers it in funeral crepe. She decides in seconds to give up mourning.

Rhett's gentlemanly social background stands him in good stead during this period. For while he disdains the social conventions, he knows them perfectly and can use them to advantage. A good example of this occurs after the bazaar when he apparently desires an invitation to Miss Pitty. Melanie had donated her beloved wedding ring to the Cause at the bazaar and, knowing her pain, Rhett redeems it at ten times its value. He immediately receives an invitation to dinner and from that time on can do no wrong in Melanie's eyes.

His blockade-running makes him a romantic figure of the times. For while he admits to Scarlett privately that it is not dangerous and that he's in it for the money, publicly he is revered for his bravery and selflessness. Gradually he is accepted into the nicer homes of Atlanta and, no sooner does this occur, than he begins to insult Atlantans with some truths about themselves couched in the politest of terms, of course. Swiftly, he is a social outcast again.

Finally in Part Two, the author reveals the war itself. The action of the battlefield is never covered directly; the reader learns what is happening through the reactions of Atlantans. It is an interesting technique because it allows exposure of important plot-developing events without a change of setting. In 1862, hopes remain high and victories are many even if people have come to realize that it will not be a short war nor an easy one. 1863 is filled with mounting disappointments and the beginning of gnawing doubts even if faith is never truly shaken. Vicksburg and Gettysburg in July are real setbacks and people begin to look grim and worried.

The real horror of war comes through only occasionally. In the author's description of the nursing that Scarlett and Melanie do, some of the terrible side-effects of war are depicted. The most touching and pathetic scene occurs in front of the newspaper office where the crowd (including Scarlett, Pitty, and Melanie), awaits the casualty sheets from Gettysburg. There is immediate tension as they search for Ashley's name and relief when it does not appear. But then the horror grows as they realize that one after another of the families around them has lost a son or lover or husband. Scarlett looks at the list again and sees not one but dozens of her childhood playmates - three of the four Tarleton boys (the fourth had been killed earlier), Raif Calvert, Joe Fontaine, Lafe Monroe. It is too much to be borne.

DISENCHANTMENT WITH WAR

This scene gives rise to one of the occasional philosophical discussions in the novel. It is not a deeply philosophical book, but through Ashley and Rhett, some views of war are elucidated. At this time Rhett tells Scarlett that there are wars because men love war. Earlier he had said that all wars are really fought over money but that the leaders make them sacred to entice people to fight in them. Such statements are totally unacceptable socially and Rhett is quickly ostracized for his remarks. Melly defends him, however, because Ashley has written her in the same vein. He sees no glory and honor in the war and knows that life will never again be the same. Ashley sees clearly that, win or lose, the South will be changed forever by this war; the old life that he once knew will be gone.

While Ashley and Rhett both mention their deeper thoughts about the war neither goes into the matter at great length. *Gone With the Wind*, as a novel, portrays the social and cultural aspects of the civilization with great depth and precision. But it does not delve deeply into the philosophical aspects of what is happening to the South. The reader is aware that Ashley has a thorough understanding of this but sees only glimpses of it. Ashley's perspectives on the society and its downfall are never brought fully to light.

Contrast In Ashley And Rhett. There are differences, too, in Rhett's and Ashley's expressions of their beliefs and these differences further delineate their characters. Rhett publicly makes known his view of the war and the Cause to the consternation of all about him. He doesn't care at all about his public image and this dims it considerably. Not only are his views on the war unacceptable, but he begins to admit publicly that his blockade-running is done for no patriotic purpose but simply to make money. And though he enrages public opinion, he manages to survive.

Ashley, on the other hand, expresses his doubts privately in letters to Melanie. He really doesn't understand why he is fighting - except perhaps to save Twelve Oaks, and the old life - but he knows that war is evil and will not preserve anything he holds dear. In this section, then, the author further clarifies the differences between those who are gentlemen and those who are not in her development of the characters of Rhett Butler and Ashley Wilkes.

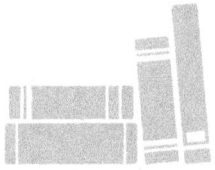

GONE WITH THE WIND

TEXTUAL ANALYSIS

PART THREE: CHAPTERS SEVENTEEN THROUGH THIRTY

IMPACT OF WAR

In Part Three of her novel, Margaret Mitchell portrays the immediate devastations of war upon a people. Scarlett O'Hara Hamilton, her heroine, is the most affected, in terms of personality, by the abrupt changes in her life. Even with the deprivations forced upon wartime Atlanta, up to the time of the siege, Scarlett had still been a pampered and petty Southern darling. Nursing in the hospital had been the most difficult thing she was asked to do and she not only shared this work with many others, she could escape it now and then and rarely missed an opportunity to do so.

SCARLETT'S GROWTH AS A PERSON

The author uses a gradual approach in Scarlett's realization that she must take the reins herself. Her first intimation of this occurs when Melly's baby is about to be born. Atlanta is in a state of siege and there are hundreds of wounded lying about the railroad depot awaiting care. Every available medical hand is needed. Scarlett fights her way through to Dr. Meade to tell him that Melly's time has come but his hands are too full of wounded and dying men. All the neighbors have evacuated. Scarlett realizes that for the first time of great need in her life she is completely alone. There is no one to whom she can turn for help. While she is grim about the fate that got her into this position, Scarlett does not run away or fail to perform. She delivers Melly's baby and gets her out of besieged Atlanta. She does what has to be done. It is a character trait that will become stronger as the story progresses.

Throughout this time of siege and difficulty Scarlett's most comforting thought is of her mother as soon as she could get home to Tara and Ellen everything would be all right. Ellen, she is sure, will know how to handle everything. Through Scarlett, Margaret Mitchell portrays beautifully what is probably a universal human trait: the desire to get someone else to share or pick up great burdens of responsibility. As capable as Scarlett proves herself to be, the desire to have someone else shoulder the burden is always there.

Thus her return to Tara with its grim facts to be faced is a horrible shock to Scarlett. As bad as conditions are, as bad as the hunger and poverty are, the worst of Scarlett's return to Tara is her inability to unload her problem on Ellen. Worse, her problems and responsibilities triple as those at Tara turn to her for answers and there is no one to whom she can turn.

STRENGTH THROUGH ADVERSITY

Adversity has a way of making some people stronger and it is a major **theme** of *Gone With the Wind* that Scarlett O'Hara is one of those people. In the face of great odds she "gets up her gumption" to defeat them. She simply refuses to allow anything to keep her down. Her life has changed abruptly. In the space of a few short days she, the pampered darling of Tara, has delivered a baby, escaped an invading army, lost her mother, seen her father reduced to mental collapse, and faced the loss of every material thing she had always taken for granted including food. Yet she refuses from the first to look back. Instead she begins work on a future in which she and her family will know no hunger. In the garden of the burned-out Twelve Oaks where she has been foraging for food, she makes her vow: she will never be hungry again. And from then on her life will be a search for the security of wealth; it will become all-important to her.

In these first days home at Tara, Scarlett's personality undergoes deep changes. Through her heroine, the author is displaying the reaction of survival against overwhelming odds. Ellen's teaching of gentleness and lady-like demeanor are forgotten in the fight against basic starvation. Scarlett is mean to the servants and vile to her sisters. But there is much work to be done if they are to remain alive and save the only thing they have left: Tara. Scarlett's sisters and Mammy and Pork rail against doing work that used to be done by lowly house-slaves and field-hands. Only Scarlett sees that life has changed irretrievably and drives the others on.

So changed is Scarlett that she can even bring herself to commit murder. A Yankee marauder breaks in on Tara when Scarlett is alone in the house with Melanie, Suellen, and Carreen - all of whom are ill - and little Wade and baby Beau. Scarlett picks up an old pistol and shoots the looter point blank. Then she and Melly steal his possessions and drag him outside to bury him before the others return.

Scarlett herself muses on how much she must have changed in order to commit this act: But the overall effect of the act is to make her stronger. In the future when facing something difficult, she will think "I've done murder, I can do this."

Scarlett again shows her determination to save Tara when a later band of Yankees comes to the plantation. Warned by a neighbor of their impending arrival, Scarlett gets all the others to hide in the swamp with as much of their food supply as possible. She intends to follow with Wade and the baby but cannot leave Tara to be burned by Sherman's men. Bravely, and alone, she faces them on the front steps. Scarlett was frightened to death by this confrontation but nothing could still her determination to save her home.

PSYCHOLOGY OF SURVIVAL

Throughout Part Three some things remain unchanged with Scarlett. She still nurtures a romantic and undying love for Ashley and occasionally resents Melly. This resentment is tempered by the fact that they are all so busy surviving that Scarlett does not have a great deal of time to waste on such matters. The author has chosen an interesting method to show the psychology of survival by having all the petty concerns of Scarlett's life before the poverty time at Tara recede against the pressing need of the moment. Only when news of Ashley's release reaches them do the old feelings flake up again. But by this time Melly has gained Scarlett's grudging respect: of them all Melanie is the only one who has accepted their fate without complaint and done what was required of her to the fullest extent of her strength. And this Scarlett must admit she admires.

MELANIE'S DEVELOPMENT

Melanie's character is more fully developed in meeting the changed circumstances of Part Three. Up to this point the author has portrayed Melanie as a true lady, gracious, charming, sweet and loyal. Her ability to see good in others because she is so good herself wins her many friends but also makes her appear silly and vulnerable at times. In fact, because of his habit, she misses a good deal of the truth of things. In the face of hard times, Melanie shows herself to be full of courage and her loyalty is stronger than ever. Never strong physically, she seems able to give her weakened body some renewed strength by sheer will power. Beau's birth is an example of this. As hope of getting the doctor or even an experienced neighbor lady trickles away, Melanie refuses to become depressed or lose courage. She experiences an exceedingly difficult labor and childbirth and Scarlett admits to herself that she would have died under such poor midwifery as she and the ignorant Prissy were able to provide. But Melanie refuses to give up. Her courage in the face of her own physical pain is amazing.

Later, at Tara, she amazes Scarlett by her reactions to the events that take place. At all times Melanie is uncomplaining and does whatever she is able in terms of physical labor to aid the survival of the family. And at crucial times she is truly wonderful. She wholeheartedly approved Scarlett's murder of the Yankee soldier and indeed, followed Scarlett down the stairs with a huge sword in hand ready to take on the marauder if necessary. It was Melanie who suggested pilfering the soldier's wallet and pockets and her chemise in which they wrapped his head so he wouldn't leave behind a trail of blood as they dragged him out of the house of his grave.

When Scarlett faces the later band of Yankees alone with Wade and Beau, it is Melanie who returns from the hiding place in the swamp to help her. Without Melanie's aid, Scarlett would have been unable to put out the fire that one of the soldiers started in the kitchen. Summoning physical strength from somewhere she and Scarlett beat at the flames with wet rugs until the fire began to die away. Then Melanie saved Scarlett's life by putting out the fire that had caught on Scarlett's back. Scarlett has to admit that Melanie is always there when she needs her.

CONTRAST IN MELANIE AND SCARLETT

While poverty has made Scarlett grasping, mean and determined to have money again, Melanie is an unselfish and sharing as ever. Sick as she is, Melanie eats less than the others and never complains (as the others do constantly) about the lack of food. When the war ends and scores of homeward-bound soldiers stop at Tara, Melanie is the one who urges the sharing of the food while Scarlett grudges them every mouthful. And when neighbor Cathleen Calvert is reduced to desperate circumstances, Scarlett is horrified that Melanie wants to offer to have her come and live at Tara.

The author does not reveal her viewpoint of the reactions of these two women to the changed circumstances of their lives. She presents Melanie's acceptance of poverty and continued unselfishness and it appears to be a good and valuable reaction. On the other hand, Miss Mitchell has Scarlett feeling, with some justification, that Melanie does not recognize the changed circumstances; that she still thinks times are like the old days when universal hospitality prevailed. Scarlett knows that times have changed. Because she is the one most responsible for survival, she sees extra guests as more mouths to feed, an idea which does not occur to Melanie. The reader is not offered a value judgment about the reactions of Melanie and Scarlett; rather the author merely lets them develop along lines peculiar to their personalities within a given set of circumstances.

REACTIONS AMONG EX-SLAVES

The rigidness of the social structure of the society which has been disrupted and torn apart by this war carries over partially into the postwar period and can be seen especially among the slaves. The situation at Tara is rapidly becoming a life-and-death one when Scarlett arrives at home but, bad as things are, she is unable to galvanize Pork and Mammy to do farm work. There is a little cotton left that needs picking and, though Scarlett herself is willing to do it, Pork and Mammy refuse. Mammy is particularly adamant - she has never been a "yard nigger," she says. She was raised in the bedroom of Ellen O'Hara's mother and now, just because Ellen is dead, she will not change the habits and status of a lifetime.

Scarlett can only occasionally get through to those at Tara that, because life has changed drastically, many of the old rules do not apply. Perhaps she is able to do it herself because she has always taken rules so lightly and broken them so easily. Scarlett accepts that life has changed, does what it necessary to survive, and worries about her code of living later. In fact, that is a characteristic reaction when faced with an unpleasant reality about herself: "I'll think about that tomorrow," she says, "tomorrow I can stand it."

Section Three as a whole provides a startling and realistic overview of the effects of war. All of the ordinary, taken-for-granted things of life are disrupted. This is shown early in the siege of Atlanta when the railroad lines are cut and later when the army commandeers the horses and buggies. The normal, accepted means of transportation are gone. Scarlett is unable to depend on these to get her back to Tara and must rely again on Rhett.

This becomes even more clear when Scarlett and Melanie reach Tara. Sherman's army, in its March to the Sea, destroyed virtually everything in its wake. For the sake of the story, the author has Tara itself spared but the food supply is done away with. It is difficult for some Americans reading this book in late twentieth-century affluence to imagine having nothing to eat and no way to get food. Yet this is the situation that faces Scarlett, and the others at Tara and the problem which they must contend with daily. Somehow, told in novel form, the effects of this war - and of all wars - become much more clear than when read of in history books. History tells us that Atlanta was embattled throughout the summer of 1864 and fell in the first week of September. Further, it says that Sherman's troops evacuated the city, stayed there until mid-November and then began the infamous "March to the Sea" at Savannah leaving a path of desolation sixty miles wide.

All this history is brought home in a keen and meaningful way when it is related by Margaret Mitchell in terms of Tara and the O'Haras. The band of Yankees that invade there and steal what little food and family treasure is to be had are terrifying and degrading in a way they could never be when spoken of in abstract terms. And in spite of her Southern bias overall, Margaret Mitchell is true to the historical events as they occurred and works the events of the novel around them.

GONE WITH THE WIND

TEXTUAL ANALYSIS

PART FOUR: CHAPTERS THIRTY-ONE THROUGH FORTY-SEVEN

MITCHELL'S USE OF HISTORICAL FACT

Part Four of *Gone With the Wind* is rich in historical detail. It shares with the rest of the work the same Southern bias in looking at history but it also draws strongly on the facts of the situation.

In the character of Archie and his dealings with Scarlett, one interesting fact of history is brought out. Before the war Archie had been a convict, incarcerated in the Milledgeville jail for forty years for the murder of his wife. At the time of the siege of Atlanta, Archie and his fellow-prisoners were released (and thereby pardoned) in order to fight for the Confederacy.

In the last desperate days of the war, exactly this had, in fact, occurred.

Later in the story Archie refuses to work for Scarlett when she leases convicts to work her sawmill. This also is based on historical fact. Economically strapped, the state of Georgia could not support its prison system. Therefore it began leasing convicts to private parties who provided the necessities for them in exchange for labor. It was a system fraught with cruelties and brutality and as it takes place in *Gone With the Wind*, Scarlett's leasing is no exception. Under Scarlett's mill manager Johnnie Gallegher, the convicts are overworked and underfed, and there is the suspicion that one is murdered. It is not a pretty picture but it is probably quite close to the truth.

The development of the Ku Klux Klan is also given some attention since Frank is killed doing its business. It is first touched upon in the novel when, shortly after Scarlett's marriage to Frank, Tony Fontaine comes to their home in the middle of the night. He has ridden hard and needs money and a new horse to get himself to Texas and away from the occupation Yankees. Tony's story opens Scarlett's eyes to a new danger in the Reconstruction South because he is running from the law. He has murdered Jonas Wilkerson who had been consorting with the freed slaves, stressing their equality and rights. When a drunken black propositions Sally Fontaine in her kitchen, Tony shoots the man and then goes after Wilkerson on the grounds that the former slave would never have thought to behave that way unless urged to by Wilkerson. In the novel this is justified, as is the formation of the Klan, by the argument that there is no law or legal authority to which white Southerners can appeal and expect to be heard fairly. There is also a very casual condoning of murder throughout this segment of the book.

The combination of an occupation army and a freed-slave class undoubtedly made life exceedingly difficult for the former white Southern aristocracy in the Reconstruction period. The author paints a grim picture of the difficulties faced by the vanquished in these times. There were the daily indignities of the Yankee occupation army and the freed slaves treating the white Southerners harshly. Much more serious in reality - if not in their own minds - was the loss of all political power. Most were disenfranchised and the legal and judicial systems were totally unresponsive to their needs. Courts frequently saw only one side of an issue and it was most often not the side of the vanquished. Finally, the concepts of justice of the white Southerner and the Carpetbaggers who held power differed greatly. Rhett Butler admits to Scarlett that he has killed a Negro because he was "uppity to a lady." That may seem just to Butler's eyes and those of his ilk, but probably wouldn't in a Carpetbagger courtroom or to the Yankee occupation army. To the reader in the second half of the twentieth century, the ease with which Rhett justifies an act of murder for so minor an offense is utterly incredible.

MITCHELL'S USE OF SCARLETT'S IGNORANCE

Scarlett's attitude toward the historical changes around her fulfills the reader's image of her character. Her selfishness persists as she takes no interest in the political changes that go on until and unless they affect her directly. In fact, the author frequently uses Scarlett's ignorance of these matters as a vehicle by which to insert explanations of them. This is most obviously the case when the legislature, still controlled by white Southerners, refuses to ratify the Fifteenth Amendment guaranteeing equal voting rights for all without regard to race. Scarlet understands nothing of this and is interested only because she is concerned about her freedom to operate her business and make money. Therefore, feeling the Yankees will force it upon them anyway, she wishes the legislature had acted differently because this will only make it more difficult for them all. Unlike many of the Old Guard, Scarlett takes no pride in the legislature's stand.

RHETT STATES THE THEME

Part Four is very important in another respect. Contained herein is the kernel paragraph expressing the basic **theme** of the entire work. Miss Mitchell uses Rhett Butler to express these important thoughts and it occurs in chapter forty-three. Rhett has returned to Atlanta a few weeks after the birth of Ella Lorena. He comes to see Scarlett to visit and tell her that he is angry because she has broken her loan agreement with him. When she borrowed the money to buy the sawmill, she promised that none should ever be used for Ashley's welfare. But now she had given Ashley half-interest in the mill and made him manager. And Rhett is coldly furious; he tells her he will not lend her more money and will see to it that she finds it hard to borrow elsewhere. After this a long discussion of Ashley occurs during which Rhett enunciates the **theme** of the book. In essence he says that the war has turned the world "upside-down." Any disaster can do it but in this case it was the war. When that happens, all people become equal again. They have only their physical strength and their brains to aid them in survival. And people like Ashley do not survive, while people like Scarlett and Rhett do. The Ashleys fail because they don't fight to survive or they don't know how. Or, even if they have the equipment to fight with, it hurts their consciences to use it. The others manage, after a time, to find their way back to the same positions they had before the upheaval. Rhett sees this simply as a law of nature and he approves of it.

This is certainly the thematic paragraph of the novel for, above all else, *Gone With the Wind* is the story of survival in troubled times and sometimes against great odds. And Miss Mitchell peoples her book with survivors and non-survivors and makes little overt judgment upon them. The reader does not come away feeling that the Scarletts and Rhetts are right and the Ashleys and Melanies are wrong or vice versa. The **theme** is more a statement of fact than a judgment of value.

Scarlett can only understand this philosophical discussion from her own point of view. She is defensive about the necessary things she had had to do in order to regain her former wealth but she does not renege on them. Instead she feels that those who hold on to honor and kindliness when they interfere with basic survival are fools. She will have time for those virtues again when she has money enough.

CONTRAST IN SCARLETT AND ELLEN

Scarlett's development in this section of the novel is to move her even further away from the teachings of her mother than ever before. Throughout the book Scarlett's image of her mother pops up to haunt her, and in the face of what she deems necessary, she represses it. Each new step that Scarlett takes she evaluates in her mother's terms and usually finds it wanting. But Scarlett consciously pushes away these thoughts of her own limitations. Always she is able to promise herself that when things are normal again she will be a great lady like Ellen. But she never realizes that being a great lady involves a kind of selflessness and kindliness and concern for others that she simply has never possessed and probably never will.

From its beginning, Part Four is fraught with courses of action that would have terrified Ellen. With her father's Irish tenacity and pride in the land, Scarlett is determined to hold on to Tara. That this may mean selling herself sexually to Rhett Butler matters little when weighed against the loss of her home. When she and Mammy arrive in Atlanta, they cross paths with Belle Watling and it occurs to Scarlett that she will be on the same footing as that despised creature when she strikes her bargain with Rhett. Even this realistic thought does not dissuade her.

At Fanny Elsing's wedding, when Scarlett is trying to ensnare Frank Kennedy, she faces another moment of truth. She is silently sneering at the poverty-stricken gentry, thinking that they ought to know better than to think they can be ladies without money. Suddenly it occurs to Scarlett that her mother would not agree with her. Ellen, like these women, would have taken pride in her poverty. But for Scarlett money is a necessary ingredient for being a lady.

Ellen O'Hara would have been horrified at Scarlett's marriage to Frank Kennedy when he was Suellen's fiance, and even more so at Scarlett's conduct within that marriage. In truth, Scarlett made Frank's life miserable. Simply, she was smarter than he about business and demonstrated it at a time in history when women were considered total muddleheads about such things. Practically from their wedding day onward, she nagged and badgered Frank about the conduct of his business, about collecting debts from old friends, about making sharper deals. And Frank allowed himself to be bullied which only whetted Scarlett's appetite.

In Scarlett's "catching" of Frank Kennedy, the author shows most clearly just how far her heroine has moved from her mother's teachings. For here was not a clear case of preference for one sister over another. That would not be in character for Scarlett; she was more ruthless than that. In conformity with her character, she blithely told Frank that Suellen had thrown him over for Tony Fontaine. Then she lived in agony for two weeks not because her conscience hurt or she feared embarrassment if Frank learned the truth; no, she was afraid a letter from Suellen would ruin her plan to save Tara.

Throughout Part Four, Scarlett's reaction to her own poverty at Tara drives her with unerring single-mindedness to her goal of obtaining money. At the same time, it is driving her further and further from the teachings of Ellen. Time and again, she blatantly transgresses social rules. She engages in business unnecessarily, appears in public while pregnant, drives her buggy unprotected around the streets, and consorts with Yankees to sell them lumber. In business she is unscrupulous and dishonest. But always she plans a return to her mother's teachings when there is money enough. She says this once to Rhett who doubts she'll make it. But Scarlett is obviously sincere in her intention to try-someday.

CHARACTERIZATION OF ASHLEY

In Part Four, the author gives the reader a better, more complete look at Ashley than in the earlier segments of the novel. Ashley sees himself as one of the weak, the nonsurvivors, as he tells Scarlett one day at Tara. He simply does not fit into the new world that has been created by the war and its aftermath. His earlier education, fine as it might have been, simply did not prepare him to do anything to ensure his own survival. Ashley seems always to be torn by his ability to see both sides of a question. This was true early in the book when he was less than enthusiastic about the South's entry into the war. And it can be seen in the section concerning the action of the legislature. While the other men are pleased and proud that the legislature refused to ratify the Fifteenth Amendment, Ashley is concerned. He does not see it in purely personal terms, like Scarlett, but questions whether it is not just a futile gesture guaranteed to bring more trouble down upon them.

Certainly Ashley displays an ambivalence in his relationship with Scarlett. He knows, realistically, that he and Melly are well suited and that Melly is about as perfect a human as one could hope for. But he seems to cherish a juvenile dream of physical possession of Scarlett that he is unable to deny. And it is on this thread of hope that Scarlett's love hangs.

Ashley seems to lack courage when it comes to decision-making. He continues to take his livelihood from Scarlett when he knows it is wrong. After having reached a decision to take a job in New York, he allows himself to be persuaded to move to Atlanta and join in the sawmill venture. He is never able to be final and definite when he tries to rebuff Scarlett's advances to him. His honesty and intelligence sometimes overwhelm his common sense.

The reader is always conscious of a side of Ashley not being explored fully. Throughout the work, it is possible to feel that all of Ashley is not being revealed, that something is left unsaid. The author does not leave her readers with a great unfulfilled desire to know more, but with the certain knowledge that there is more to be known.

SOCIAL CHANGE DRAMATIZED

Finally there are interesting social accommodations which take place in Part Four. The War Between the States deprived the South (and the North as well) of a whole generation of its young men. That is a fact which is understood much better when told through a novel than through history, and Margaret Mitchell brings it home by picturing the plight of Suellen O'Hara. So many of the County's young men have been killed that there is virtually no one left for Suellen and girls like her to marry. Will Benteen, the young "Cracker" soldier who recovered his health at Tara after the war, becomes acceptable under these circumstances. His small-farmer background and lack of formal education, combined with a virtual lack of traceable ancestry, would have rendered him totally unacceptable before the war. He would not have come near Tara. In the post-bellum period, however, his honesty and ability to get things done are welcome assets. People of "breeding," like Grandma Fontaine and Mrs. Tarleton, regret that the situation has forced Scarlett to accept Will as Suellen's husband, but are grateful that such men are available. It is an extension of the philosophy and **theme** that Rhett expresses in his conversation about survival. The upheaval has made Suellen and Will equal. Some may regret it but, in a way, it appears to have improved the grounds for choice. Will is accepted, even with his lack of sparkle, on the basic grounds of his virtue and capability, with considerations of "background" pushed aside by necessity.

Other changes are reflected in Atlanta society and frequently based on the same lack of available young men. Some of the girls just a generation younger than Scarlett are faced with the same scarcity of beaux as Suellen. And the beaux they have are poverty-stricken, serious and driven to hard work unlike the young men of the antebellum period. Less bitter and loyal than their older sisters (since they were little girls during the war), some of this generation begin to mingle with the well-dressed, handsome soldiers of the Yankee garrison. Marriages are made. But unlike the case of Will Benteen and his type, this sort of husband is unacceptable. And this type of marriage creates hard and bitter rifts in Southern families. The suspicion arises that another generation or two must pass before the bitterness will fade and acceptance follow. But for this period of the novel, these marriages reflect an interesting fact of history and social reaction within the framework of the fictional tale.

GONE WITH THE WIND

TEXTUAL ANALYSIS

PART FIVE: CHAPTERS FORTY-EIGHT THROUGH SIXTY-THREE

SOCIAL AND PERSONAL HISTORY COMBINED

Part Five of *Gone With the Wind* is really two things: it is a social history of the second period of Southern Reconstruction and it is a finalization of the personal histories of Margaret Mitchell's highly realistic characters.

As social history *Gone With the Wind* introduces the reader again to the various types of people who inhabit the area and upon whose interaction the story depends.

The Old Guard is the bulwark of Atlanta society at this point. It consists of white Southerners who were socially prominent before the war and who defended the Cause with all their hearts. The Elsings, Meades, Merriwethers, Whitings, all are there - but life has changed for them. They have lost two important things: money and power. All of these people now live in a kind of genteel poverty hacking out a living as best they can: Rene Picard and Grandpa Merriwether ride a pie wagon selling Mrs. Merriwether's baked goods and they are very successful. Hugh Elsing works for Scarlett at the sawmill and he is not very successful. But all live with a pride in their poverty and in their Lost Cause that puzzles and annoys Scarlett. And their ideas of correct behavior now revolve around loyalty to the Cause and unrelenting bitterness toward the former foe. Those forced by their poverty to become Republicans are simply cast out. And any consorting with Scallawags, Republicans, Carpetbaggers or members of the Yankee Garrison is enough to make one persona non grata in most "nice" Atlanta homes.

MASTERFUL PICTURE OF CARPETBAGGERS

The Carpetbaggers with whom Scarlett associates have come to Reconstruction Georgia from various places. They hope to profit by manipulating politics and office-holding while Georgia's government is out of the hands of her own people. Margaret Mitchell does a masterful job of presenting them. Largely, they are people who have traveled extensively just on the wrong side of the law. For example, when Scarlett becomes pregnant with Bonnie, one of her new friends, Mamie Bart, tells her that there are things that can be done to get rid of an unwanted pregnancy. Rhett explodes with anger pointing out that this clearly exhibits Mamie's origins as madam of a brothel and makes Scarlett promise to have her baby.

Miss Mitchell, with some fairness, points out that there were many legitimate Northerners who came South to make their homes after the war but who quickly turned their backs on the trashy profiteering kind of Carpetbagger. Presumably these good people were more acceptable to the Old Guard than the Scallawags or turncoat Southerners.

There were many Southern soldiers who were in great need in this period. They and their families were frequently on the edge of starvation. Often their only hope was to turn Republican and rejoin the political structure to enable them to get jobs or help from the government. These Scallawags, as they were known, were held in utter contempt by the Old Guard who felt that they, too, were suffering but would never give in to those in power.

These were the people Scarlett took to her breast, and, in doing so, cut herself off from her old friends. Worst of all she befriended the hated Governor Bullock, a Republican elected through disenfranchisement of white Southerners and scandalous election practices. Scarlett befriended these people because they were fun and had money to have fun with. Also, she could be arrogant and bully them and they would return because she was the only member of the Old Guard who would have anything to do with them. Furthermore, she wished to keep political pressure off her businesses. For her, it was expedient to go along and get along. To the rest of Atlanta, it was unforgivable.

Through Scarlett's association with these people, Miss Mitchell allows her readers to see the rounded picture of Atlanta's social and political life in the post-war era. It is in the development of their personal lives, however, that the interest really lies. All of the major relationships in the book reach as denouement in Part Five. And each of the characters sees things about himself and others that he had not seen before.

RHETT AND SCARLETT AT CROSS-PURPOSES

Rhett and Scarlett's relationship is unendingly interesting. Through Part Five they seem to be at cross purposes. Scarlett has always desired to make Rhett love her so that she can hold it over his head as she has done with all her other beaux. But he consistently denies that he loves her, merely stating that he wants her physically. The alert reader can decipher his love in many places. His declaration to Scarlett on the road to Tara during the siege and his frustration at not being able to help her when she came to him in jail are but two examples. Also Scarlett often notices how he looks at her with a waiting, patient look, never realizing that he loves her desperately and is waiting for her to love him.

MITCHELL'S ORCHESTRATION OF MISSED OPPORTUNITIES

Then there is Rhett's reaction to Ashley. It is not just that Rhett views him as one of the non-survivors of the upheaval they have all experienced. More than that there is a passionate, if reined, bitterness in Rhett's reaction to Ashley. This is clear even on the Butlers' honeymoon when he leaves Scarlett's bed and stays away for a day because he has caught her sighing over thoughts of Ashley. On the night of Ashley's birthday party, when Rhett arouses passion in Scarlett that she has never known, he admits that he loves her. When he returns they face a moment in which Scarlett's budding love might have bloomed but Rhett's off-hand denial of his love arouses her pride and they quarrel again. They face another such moment when Scarlett miscarries. Had she only ignored her pride and called for him, as she wanted to, things might have been different. But Miss Mitchell orchestrates these missed opportunities beautifully so that the suspense never wavers.

It becomes clear as the relationship between Scarlett and Rhett progresses that Rhett transfers a great deal of his feeling for Scarlett to Bonnie. He wants to pet and spoil Scarlett, to indulge her every whim and enjoy her hard and grasping nature. When Scarlett denies him this (after having provided him it earlier in their marriage), Rhett begins to treat Bonnie the same way. He spoils her recklessly and indulges her completely until she is truly a very difficult child to handle. Ultimately this leads to her death because the pony is a direct result of this indulgence. And it creates an even wider breach between Bonnie's mother and father.

In this final section, Rhett and Scarlett both learn things they have not known before. Rhett faces the fact that his love for Scarlett has died. For so long he has cared so very much and watched Scarlett covertly for any sign of returned affection. He did not allow his love to show because Scarlett was so cruel and heartless to all who loved her. But the fascination has worn off with the years and now he cannot remember why he cared so much. Rhett also acknowledges a change within himself. He wants to return to some of the old values that he has cast aside. The cheap and shoddy associations of his present life have palled and he thinks he can find some meaning in his old life.

SCARLETT'S INSIGHTS

Scarlett faces more realities than any of the other characters. She finally sees that the basic beliefs she has had about her whole life are all confused. When Melanie dies, Scarlett sees Ashley in a new and more truthful light for the first time. She finally realizes that the Ashley she has loved for so long existed only in her imagination. As a very young girl she had an image of a dream lover and she made Ashley fit that image. But in reality Ashley has never been there when she needed him or helped her through anything serious. But always there was Rhett. Rhett had helped her through almost every bad moment of her life.

Scarlett also views Melanie in a new way. Melanie's likeness to Ellen becomes clear for the first time when Scarlett sees that

Melanie is the only woman friend she ever had. And Melly has stood by Scarlett unendingly. From the most serious life-and-death moments when they faced starvation and the Yankees to the social disasters in which Scarlett embroiled herself, Melanie has been there helping to fend off the world and keep Scarlett safe. But it is not until Melly's death that Scarlett realizes this and admits her dependence on another person.

Ashley, like Scarlett, finally accepts the truth of his own love for Melanie, but only as she lies dying. Finally his lusting after Scarlett is seen for what it really is and Melly's worth becomes concrete to him. Scarlett berates him for not having known sooner and for dangling her along with delicate admissions of love combined with talk of honor and sacrifice. But he is truly helpless without Melanie and Scarlett realizes that she will always have to take care of him like a child because she promised Melanie.

Of them all only Melanie escapes the realization of life being very different from the way she conceived it. She has loved and trusted them all, refused to see the worst in them and made the best much better than it was. Mercifully, the author allows her to die without discovering the truth.

All of this self-realization is completely in character for this kind of novel for, above all, *Gone With the Wind* is a romantic tale of exciting people living out their lives in a thrilling time. Having set her story against such a background, the author makes excellent use of the history of the times and in doing so, exposes readers to much of it in a new and refreshing way. But mostly, it is a readable and exciting story, in which highly real characters test their ability to survive in a time in which all men are so tested.

GONE WITH THE WIND

CHARACTER ANALYSES

SCARLETT O'HARA

Scarlett O'Hara was bred to be a far different person from the one Rhett leaves at the end of the story. She should have been a loved and sheltered Southern lady, the mistress of a great plantation, a paragon of good breeding and good taste. Her Mammy and her mother bent themselves sincerely to the task of building such an individual and but for two factors they might have succeeded. Those two factors were Scarlett's own personality and the Civil War.

Scarlett's personality was a difficult one to work with, if you desired, as Ellen and Mammy did, to create a self-effacing, genteel lover of humanity. Scarlett was by nature too willful and selfish, too direct in her approach to life to fit into the mold designed for her. She had too much honesty to employ the dissembling required of a lady except when it suited her to do so. While not honest in a truth-telling sense, she viewed the world in an honest light, although she often hid this from public view. The author provides for a great deal of dramatic tension in the dynamics which develop between Scarlett's own personality and the one it is desired that she acquires.

And then there was the war. It provided a perfect testing-ground against which the characters in the novel would be tried. And Scarlett is tested in the greatest depth and detail. From a cushioned, sheltered, pampered life which has avoided all training in the basics of life, she is thrown into a real struggle for survival. The war provides a perfect means by which to do this, and the struggle of Scarlett and the others in turn elucidates the war.

Scarlett's relationship to Ashley Wilkes is a motivating force throughout the novel. It is frequently the cause of major events while, in itself, it is almost a non-relationship. Certainly it is influenced definitively by both Scarlett's personality and the Civil War.

Scarlett falls in love with Ashley when she is fifteen years old. He seems to fill best the image of a lover she has created for herself and, as important, he has not succumbed to her charms as all the other County boys have. There is frequently present the idea that Ashley is as much of a challenge as anything else.

Because of certain personality traits of Scarlett's this cherished love does not wear off. Scarlett's poor judgment never rights until the end of the novel. She is unable to judge people for their real qualities and Ashley is foremost among the misjudged. The author points out that Scarlett is shocked when, after Ashley takes over running the mill, he does not immediately make a profitable venture of it. Yet the fact that he would be unable to do well at it is perfectly clear to everyone else.

Scarlett's stubborn streak does little to improve the situation. After the war every encounter between Scarlett and Ashley has Scarlett feeling frustrated, irritated or annoyed with him. Yet she cannot admit that he is not living up to the glowing dream she has built. Also, Scarlett's stubborn clinging to the dream is fed by Ashley's inability to deny that, in some way, he loves her. Whether it is purely carnal desire, as Scarlett assumes in the end, or something a little deeper, the reader never quite knows. But it is difficult to suppress the wish for Ashley to deny any attraction because it is clear that Scarlett would survive such a denial and move on without a blind and foolish passion holding her back. This is, of course, another example of the author's setting of dramatic tension which compels involvement on the reader's part.

In addition to Scarlett's personality, the war had a profound effect on the relationship between these two characters. In the first place, they were separated for long periods of time which disallowed the possibility of more knowledge of each other. If Scarlett had been thrown together with Ashley on a regular basis early in their relationship, she might have seen the truth about his personality. But the war intervenes and by the time they are together Scarlett has created an imaginary Ashley so glorious that the real one rarely penetrates the image.

And the war tended, as wars do, to romanticize the situation. There is a tone of glory about it. And while Scarlett is, in her own mind, anything but a sentimental Confederate, she is moved by the sight of Ashley in uniform and worries incessantly over his whereabouts and state of health. Also the idea of Ashley returning in some future time helps Scarlett through her lowest moments at Tara. She is always able to visualize a sugary future in which she will be with Ashley and all will be perfect.

Scarlett's realistic relationship with a man is with Rhett Butler and again her lack of judgment plays a major role. She can never see that Rhett's actions speak louder than his denials and that he is madly in love with her. She misses completely the fact that from the time they met in Atlanta, she has always had Rhett to fall back on. And Scarlett, until the very end, sees only that Rhett is a scamp and fails to notice the enormous good of which he is capable.

Again, also, her stubbornness interferes with a relationship. Toward the end of the novel, Miss Mitchell utilizes the stubbornness with which she has endowed her heroine to create a great deal of tension and involvement. When Scarlett miscarries, for example, Rhett waits outside her door for her call. And Scarlett wants to call for him but her stubborn pride interferes. Prior to this **episode**, when she has told Rhett that he is no longer welcome in her bedroom, she regrets her hasty action. But stubbornness and pride again block healing progress and they remain apart.

In spite of her poor judgment which glorifies Ashley and diminishes Rhett, Scarlett has a tremendous survival instinct and this returns her to Rhett at regular intervals in the story. When Tara is in jeopardy she swallows her pride to find Rhett in the Atlanta jail. She borrows money from him to buy the sawmill and it is Rhett to whom she confesses her guilt and anguish over Frank's death. It is this instinct combined with a strong sense of responsibility to her own family that leads her to marry Frank Kennedy and, probably, to marry Rhett. When starving at Tara, Scarlett rejects the idea of farming the family out to others. She will take care of her own because that is what the O'Haras do. And with marriage to Rhett she assures herself enough money to do it properly to her way of thinking.

Rhett and Scarlett are really perfect foils for one another. They look at the world in much the same way, shunning idealism and honor as motivating forces and pursuing selfish, interesting goals. The author has them meet against a background of excitement and shifting social orders, which would test their ability to survive and break new social ground. Scarlett and Rhett do both.

In Scarlett O'Hara, Margaret Mitchell has created the ultimate survivor. She is greedy, avaricious, immoral. She is female in a time when her sex so seriously limited her survival options that it is a miracle she made it at all. And she is single-minded to the point that she is really blind to all but her own goals. So Scarlett does survive. She survives an upheaval of society which has destroyed most of the people she knew. She provides materially for relatives better than anyone else she knows. But she also loses. At the close of *Gone With the Wind* Scarlett has lost every single thing she ever cared about except Tara. And her own personality is at fault. Her single-minded stubbornness has provided her with the things she set out for but lost her the things that were really important to her.

Finally, *Gone With the Wind* closes with Scarlett's enigma: does she win back Rhett's love? Margaret Mitchell always said she didn't know and with the personality she built for Scarlett O'Hara it is possible to postulate both kinds of answers. Certainly it has always been one of the most tantalizing questions confronting readers of this exciting, thoroughly American novel.

RHETT BUTLER

Rhett Butler, the major male figure of *Gone With the Wind*, initially seems to be a perfect stereotype of the villain down to his piercing, dark eyes and black moustache. His reputation fulfills the promise of his appearance by casting him in an even darker role. And, to finish the picture, his opening act, as eavesdropper to Scarlett's most embarrassing, unladylike moment, makes his villainy complete.

But to cross him off as a type-cast villain is to do the author and her character an injustice. For here is no flat, one-dimensional figure, playing a single role. Instead, Miss Mitchell presents a rounded human being with warmth and honesty as well as flaws and imperfections. It is to her credit as an author that she is able to create so living, so believable a character as Rhett Butler.

Though a self-proclaimed scamp and profiteer, Rhett Butler has deep wells of goodness and decency which his actions proclaim. Some of these virtues appear in his relationship with Melanie Wilkes. Although he is aware of many truths that would hurt Melanie deeply if she knew them, he carefully shields her from them. While he uses the truth maliciously with Scarlett and, more especially, her Scallawag friends, he is extremely careful of Melanie's feelings and illusions about her life. His adoration of Bonnie Blue and kindness to Scarlett's other children is further demonstration of his basic decency. Rhett loves children and is much more tolerant of them and their ways than is Scarlett. And when he can no longer spoil and pet his wife, he transfers this indulgence to Bonnie, with an open adoration that endears him to many who previously thought ill of him.

On character trait of Rhett's which encourages ill will is his ability to see through the pretensions and illusions of others and his inability or unwillingness to keep silent about them. Even in his opening appearance in the novel, at Wilkes' barbecue, he is using the truth against illusion and making himself unpopular. When he points out that the North is much better prepared for war and that this will be no easy victory, the blood of every loyal Confederate rises. In fact, what he says is true, but the saying of it in a social setting is unnecessary. It is a performance to be repeated many times during the war in Atlanta. Dr. Meade is an especially fine target for such polite home truths.

The author gives Rhett a background which somewhat explains this social iconoclasm. His ostracism from society at an early age has hurt him more deeply than he usually shows. It is demonstrated really only once in a conversation with Scarlett after the birth of Ella. He feels that he owes nothing to a society which abandoned him and so spends a good deal of his time pointing out its pretensions.

In spite of this rejection of the society that denied him, Rhett is aware of its virtues. We see this in his relationship with Melanie. Rhett is always kind to her because he recognizes her goodness. Ideally, Melanie is what all ladies should be. She is guided by virtuous motives without being sickeningly sweet, and she sees the good so regularly that often people behave better as a result of it. Rhett does not share these traits but he is able to recognize and appreciate their value.

Finally his appreciation of his heritage is demonstrated in his quixotic joining of the Confederate army as it leaves Atlanta. Even Rhett is amused by this action and hardly understands it himself. But that is part of the credibility of Margaret Mitchell's characterization. Sometimes the people she has created, like real human beings, do not understand or cannot articulate their own motivations. It is one of the reasons her characters live, outside the novel, in the readers' imaginations.

Another of Rhett's character traits is his great ability to manipulate others. He goes in and out of favor in Atlanta practically at will, alternately alienating and charming the town's most stiff-necked citizens. Early in the war he gains great favor as the dashing and courageous blockader. This makes it easy for Scarlett to see him even though he is not received elsewhere in the South. Once he feels secure that Scarlett will see him no matter what his reputation, he sheds his heroic robes and begins puncturing holes in the vanity and hypocrisy of the proper gentry who idolize him. Soon he is received no where but Aunt Pittypat's, a condition which persists until long after the war.

Rhett's saving of the gentlemen of Atlanta by having Belle Watling and her girls provide an alibi for them again gains him an unwilling reception in Atlanta. After the Butlers' honeymoon, people come to call because he has saved lives, but they do not like it. And the Butlers' continued travels with Carpetbaggers and Scallawags earns again the town's hatred.

Only after the birth of Bonnie does Rhett try to regain his reputation. This he does with relative ease by joining the Democratic Party and contributing to the proper causes. He even resorts to bragging about his war record. His manipulation of the affections of almost everyone he knows is complete. Scarlett is the lone exception and he does manage to manipulate her actions most of the time. But he cannot make her love him and the suspense of his attempt contributes enormously to the readability of the novel.

Of all the characters, Rhett seems to be the author's favorite for use as a "mouthpiece" to comment on the social scene or on a deeper, more philosophical plane. He is constantly pointing out the foibles of society; indeed, to do so almost seems a major thrust of his life, Rhett often appears to live at the edges of things, observing them, commenting on them, but never really participating in them. Certainly this is true of his unspoken love of Scarlett; he is always keeping his emotions on a tight rein with her.

On a deeper level, Rhett is the character who most frequently repeats the major **theme** of the work: that, in disasters, all in society become equal and start over. When they do, some survive and succeed, others merely survive, and some go under completely. Rhett is clearly a survivor and a succeeder. Twice in his life he has seen the world upturn. Once, at age twenty, when he was turned away without a penny for disgracing his family. And once again when the Civil War ended the old order. Both times Rhett, by his wits and charm, has come out on top, and he has an ill-concealed contempt for those who cannot make it.

The author also uses Rhett, perhaps because he is so often outside the bounds of society, to comment on the deeper meanings of life. For example, Rhett and Ashley are the only two characters who read any philosophical meaning into the Civil War and move from it to comment on war in general. Other characters spout stereotypical views about the Cause and the War and honor and glory. But Ashley and, perhaps even more so, Rhett, see through the trappings and come closer to the reality of the conflict.

In sum, Rhett Butler is an immensely interesting character who begins as a stereotype but flourishes into one of the most believable and bewitching of the figures who people American literature.

MELANIE WILKES

Melanie Hamilton Wilkes is a character who is so good that she is almost, but not quite, unbelievable. She has one quality that draws all who know her to her side: she always sees the good in people. Even in the most unredeemable slave, Melly would find one good quality and magnify it until that person might even begin to live up to it. Melanie is like this for several reasons. For one thing she is a warm and generous person who cannot bear to see those around her unhappy. One of the swiftest ways to alleviate unhappiness is to begin to notice and mention virtues of the unhappy person. This habit is second nature to Melanie. And she never uses it (as Scarlett does), to gain her own ends but always to seek the comfort of others. Another reason Melanie sees so much good is that she has so little knowledge of evil. Raised by Aunt Pitty under the supervision of Uncle Peter in the house on Peachtree Street, Melly has had no chance to be acquainted with the evils of the world. Having lost her parents at an early age, she was not even exposed to the normal tensions of a marriage. In that house, people deferred quietly to each other's opinions and little of the world intruded. Having such a small acquaintance with duplicity and evil, she never assumes that these lie behind anyone's actions. For example, when Rhett returns her wedding ring after the hospital benefit, Melanie sees it as an exceedingly thoughtful act by a generous and kindly man. It never occurs to her that there could be an ulterior motive. Yet Scarlett knows that he wants an invitation to Aunt Pitty's and that he has chosen a certain way to obtain it.

But for all her naivete and idealization of people, Melanie does exhibit a certain basic common sense which even a grudging Scarlett has to admire. One such occasion occurs at the hospital bazaar when the Home Guard marches for the assembled guests. Melly's sturdily expressed opinion that the able-bodied young men of the group ought to be at the front startles all who hear it. It makes a great deal of sense but it is so unlike Melanie to say anything that might hurt feelings that her listeners can hardly believe it. It is just this kind of **episode** which delineates what a talented architect of character Margaret Mitchell is. Melanie's little outbursts of common sense are somewhat out of character but real human beings occasionally behave in an "out-of-character" fashion. It is a fine hand that can draw people who are out of character enough to be real but not so much that they lose credibility.

Melanie continues this pattern when it is she who, after Scarlett's "debut" at the bazaar, takes a much more sensible view of the custom of mourning than her fellow matrons. Partly this is in defense of Scarlett's unladylike behavior but also it arises out of the logic of the situation. It is wartime, after all, and it is somewhat ridiculous for the Hamilton house to be shut against the outside world when there are so many lonely soldiers who could use the company or convalescents who need a place to stay.

Later, toward the end of the story, Melanie defends Scarlett's working and running the mills on a common-sense basis. Scarlett is smart about business and in desperate times, the smart must work at whatever is available. She sees the older matrons' hatred of Scarlett as jealousy of her success. This is somewhat unrealistic but it does contain an important kernel of truth.

Another of Melanie's sterling qualities is that she always seems to be there when those who love her need her. She works against a handicap in this, for she is a physically weak person, especially after the birth of Beau. Scarlett discovers this while they are at Tara together and years later learns that she has depended on it all along. At Tara, not only did Melly uphold Scarlett's authority on a daily basis but she alone was there when the major crisis occurred. When the lone Yankee came to loot Tara and Scarlett shot him, it was Melanie who stood at the top of the stairs ready to go after him with Charles' sword.

And when Sherman's men looted and set fire to Tara, Melanie returned from hiding in the swamp just in time to help Scarlett keep Tara from burning.

Melanie has a stubbornness about her loyalties which has both good and bad aspects. Once she makes up her mind about a person she can rarely be persuaded to change it. And usually, she makes it up on the positive side.

She is stubbornly, fiercely defensive about Scarlett in spite of overwhelming evidence indicating the heroine. Melanie would never forget how kind and good Scarlett had been to her during Beau's birth and after the siege, at Tara. Even when Scarlett was caught in the act of embracing Ashley, Melanie refused to believe. More than that she cast Ashley's sister, India, out of her life for telling such a tale. Only the deepest kind of loyalty could have allowed Melanie to precipitate so distasteful a family feud.

Toward the end of the novel, the author begins to view Melanie as a type, a paradigm of Southern womanhood, stubbornly loyal to the Lost Cause, and implacable in her hatred of the foe. It is a kind of stubborn loyalty that is always linked with extreme patriotism but it does little to heal the wounds of war.

An example of this fierce hate occurs when Melanie questions Scarlett's consorting with Carpetbaggers and Yankees. She does not understand how Scarlett can do it because her own hatred is so strong. She fully intends to teach her children and grandchildren to hate Yankees. It is this very kind of stubbornness, which some see as admirable national loyalty, that keeps the fires of war burning. Melly, in her implacable hatred, is unable to see the spirit of peace, healing and reconciliation as good goals. And if Margaret Mitchell was correct in her estimation, there was a whole generation just like Melanie.

ASHLEY WILKES

George Ashley Wilkes has a certain kind of intellectuality and view of life that sets him apart from the other County young men who come calling at Tara. The Wilkeses are all characterized by a love of books and music that makes them unique among County folk. They take Grand Tours of Europe and travel north to New York to visit museums and see plays. Ashley and his family escape the derision of their neighbors for their artiness only because they are so well accomplished in things that County people feel are important. Ashley can outride and outshoot anybody in the area. He has a good head for whiskey and he gambles competently. The fact that his heart is not fully committed to these pastimes is overlooked because he does them so well.

Ashley's love of things of the mind divorces him somewhat from the more mundane things of earth. This detachment creates an ambivalence about Ashley that may be his most outstanding characteristic. He sees so many sides of so many issues that he often finds action difficult.

Ashley experiences confusion about the war and seemingly about his attachment to Scarlett. The only thing he knows for sure that he wants is for the old way of life to return. He wants the leisure to spin his dreams and hear his music and pay as little attention as possible to the everyday things about him. It is his inability to deal with his attachment to Scarlett that is one of the major points of interest and conflict in the story. From the long days in the County before the war through the awful period of Reconstruction, Ashley constantly struggles with himself about Scarlett. This struggle only surfaces for the reader's attention periodically but it seems to give Ashley a good deal of trouble. The conflict seems to be that Ashley sees in Scarlett all the fire and passion for life that he can never feel. He is enormously attracted to her physically but he knows that any union between them would be very unhappy because they are so different. Scarlett would never understand his intellectual pursuits and would grow increasingly impatient with them. But Ashley, in spite of this knowledge, can never manage to deny to Scarlett his love for her. He either has a fierce passion for truth-telling or perhaps in some unexplained way he enjoys keeping Scarlett dangling. Whatever the reason (which the reader never learns), the result is the same. Scarlett clings madly to every shred of evidence of his love when it is clear that her pride and dignity would salvage her if that love were denied outright to her.

This is especially true toward the end of the novel when Scarlett's inability to see clearly leads to such tragic consequences. If, at Tara, after the war, Ashley had simply lied and denied his attraction it seems likely that Scarlett would have survived and perhaps achieved a true alliance with Rhett. It is a great credit to Margaret Mitchell's skill as a designer of plot and a builder of character that she so carefully interplays the intricacies of her plot line with the flaws and foibles of her characters. It is what makes her work so eminently readable.

The characteristic of Ashley's that contributes most heavily to defining the main **theme** of the book is that he cannot survive the calamitous changes that have rocked them all. In a novel about survival, Ashley is the author's most well-defined example of a person who is not going to make it. He was prepared to live in a different kind of world - a world in which all of his material needs and daily wants were attended to. It was a world which gave him all the leisure that he needed for dreaming and thinking and in which he never had to confront the realities of life. And Ashley fit into it very well. But that world is gone and in the upheaval, all are equal. To succeed, to achieve any kind of leisure, he must compete and fight and get down to bitter human realities. And he cannot do it. He cannot do it when Tara is about to be lost and Scarlett goes off to sell herself to a man she does not love. And he cannot do it when he runs the sawmill and never learns even the basics of the business. Only with Melanie's death does Scarlett learn what Ashley is and how much protection from the world he needs.

There are those critics who have said that for *Gone With the Wind* to have achieved the status of great literature, Ashley's character needed to have been drawn in greater depth and detail. No character sees the events that occur with enough depth and perspective, they say, to make it qualify as a great work of art. And only Ashley, with his intellectual bent, might have thrown a deeper, more penetrating light on these events.

As it is the reader does get glimpses of Ashley's views which are far from what the average Confederate is thinking. In a letter to Melanie, he points out that he doesn't really know why he is fighting, except perhaps to save an old way of life that he is sure is gone anyway. But he abhors violence and certainly does not fight for any of the reasons that his neighbors do.

Later, when Scarlett defends her use of leased convict labor at the mills by pointing out to Ashley that he owned slaves, he says that he would have freed them all when his father died. Although he immediately protests that convict labor is different and harsher than slave ownership, his admission that he would have freed the slaves is the only indication in the whole book that any white Southerner ever had second thoughts about the slave system. Certainly a pursuit of this thought in Ashley's mind would have opened new vistas in *Gone With the Wind*.

GERALD O'HARA

Gerald O'Hara, husband of Ellen and father of Scarlett, was the parent from whom Scarlett took most of her characteristics. At one point, Rhett Butler refers to him as a "Mick on the make," but even Rhett would have been the first to admit that Gerald O'Hara was the type to be among the survivors of a disaster. That he did not survive the war and its aftermath is due largely to his great dependence upon Ellen in his later life. Had the disaster of the war occurred earlier in his life, it is difficult to imagine his failure to survive it.

Forced to leave Ireland for political trouble with the English law, he had come to America with virtually nothing in his pocket. Although he was welcome to stay on with his tradesmen brothers in Savannah, with whom he had done very well, Gerald hungered after more. He felt strongly the lack of social status attached to tradesmen and he resolved to do something about it. Perhaps in Gerald's ambition and spirit of competitiveness, the author is demonstrating two of the characteristics which contribute to the make-up of people who survive upheaval. Certainly Gerald had these in abundance.

Just as his daughter in later years would use her talents to their best advantage when she wanted something, so Gerald, in trade in Savannah, put his abilities to good use. His head for whiskey and his skill at cards were to serve Gerald well in his quest for the social status of plantation ownership. He obtains his valet, Pork, his first slave, and later, his plantation, Tara, by judicious use of poker and whiskey.

When Gerald sets his heart on a lady of breeding for a wife, neither his poker playing nor his head for whiskey can help him. His supreme self-confidence and conviction that he is as good as any man enable him to pay court to the elegant Ellen Robillard without fear. But it is a pure stroke of luck for Gerald that Ellen is at this time broken-hearted and desires estrangement from her family. Otherwise his chances of such a marriage at such a time and place would have, indeed, been poor.

After his marriage to Ellen, Gerald reaches the pinnacle of his dreams. He no longer needs the ambition and competitiveness that have driven him in younger years because he has achieved so much of what he had set out to achieve. Gerald did not even need to keep his wits sharpened to maintain his property because now he has Ellen who manages his property and his life for him in the tacit manner befitting her station.

So, for twenty years he depends on Ellen, is led by her decisions, and devotes himself to ease and pleasure. The qualities of strength and true aggressiveness seem to ebb with lack of use so that when Ellen dies, there is nothing left for Gerald. He is old and he has not used his strengths in so long that he seems unable to. His mind wanders and he is never again to be the same man he was before her death.

ELLEN O'HARA

It is from Ellen Robillard O'Hara that Scarlett takes her strain of "good blood" and her fleeting ambition to be a great lady. For Ellen is a great lady in the same way that Melanie Wilkes is and Scarlett does not really understand what this means until after Melanie's death.

Ellen Robillard comes from a long line of wealthy and powerful people and she has been raised according to a code which she believes in and to which she will adhere all her life. In the years in which the reader sees her at Tara, Ellen is calm, stately, humorless, and never angry. It is difficult to imagine that her marriage to Gerald came about through both anger and revenge, yet this, the author says in flashback, is exactly the case. For Ellen's marriage to Gerald began in a way not too dissimilar to Scarlett's marriage to Charles Hamilton.

Ellen was deeply and passionately in love with a cousin named Philippe Robillard. Apparently he was a wild and unsettled youth and unacceptable to Ellen's family for they manage to see that he is sent West. In doing this they hope to remove Ellen from the danger of a mismatch but the result is far different from what they expect. Philippe is killed in a brawl shortly thereafter and Ellen is filled with bitterness and the desire for revenge. At this time Gerald has proposed to her and in an angry desire to get back at her family and away from Savannah, she accepts him. Gerald with his lack of family is less acceptable than was Philippe but Ellen forces her father's hand. A staunch Protestant, he yields to the threat that if she is not permitted to marry Mr. O'Hara, she will enter the convent. From this one **episode** it is possible to see that Scarlett did not inherit all her impulsiveness and stubbornness from her father. It was there in Ellen, too, however well hidden in later years. But Ellen was a truly great lady. Gerald O'Hara was never to know the reason for his good fortune and Ellen treated him with dignity, love, and devotion throughout their marriage. It she ran things and made decisions, he was never to feel slighted for she completely hid the fact that she was the power at Tara. Her religion and background had not led her to expect happiness in this life and she never showed Gerald if she felt its lack. It is hard to imagine that Scarlett would have treated her impulsively chosen Charles in the same manner, had he lived.

MAMMY

The character of Mammy, as portrayed by Margaret Mitchell, is a highly stereotyped version of the black slave mistress of the Old South. She is romanticized and one-dimensional. Her thoughts and concerns are totally concentrated on the O'Haras. Only once in the entire novel do Mammy's thoughts turn to herself and that occurs when, at Tara in wartime, Scarlett wants them all to pick cotton. This does not fit at all with Mammy's idea of the social scheme of things and she refuses outright.

Mammy accepts her place in life without question. After the war, when other blacks take advantage of their new freedom, she considers them "trashy." Her concept of the social system is as rigid as the system itself and she spares no one her view when she feels it is being abrogated. Indeed, she not only oversees the social behavior of the O'Hara girls but in later years it is Mammy to whom Rhett turns when he wants to know the proper behavior for Bonnie.

Mammy's relationship to Rhett develops along interesting lines. At first she is filled with contempt for such trash. She even insists on accompanying Scarlett to Atlanta when she suspects (correctly), that Scarlett will try to get the money to save Tara from "dat rapscallion Butler man."

Mammy counsels Scarlett against marrying Rhett and refuses to wear the red taffeta petticoat he brings her from New Orleans. She calls him "Cap'n Butler" instead of the more familial "Mist' Rhett." It is not until she lives with the Butlers for a while, under the softening influence of his charm, that she weakens toward Rhett. On the day of Bonnie Blue's birth, when Rhett is so genuinely thrilled with the arrival of a daughter, Mammy yields completely. She puts on the red petticoat and from then on he is "Mist' Rhett."

Mammy's relationship with Scarlett is usually tense for she is always eagle-eyed about Scarlett's generally disapproved behavior. Only when Scarlett goes after Frank Kennedy does Mammy, overlooking Suellen's rights, give her full approval. She is a realist and sees Scarlett in trouble and seeking an acceptable, if sticky, solution.

Late in the novel Mammy returns to Tara, unable to tolerate the depths to which this loved child of Ellen has fallen.

PORK

Pork is Gerald O'Hara's valet and the first slave the Irishman owned. He was won by Gerald in a poker game in Savannah and was Gerald's first step toward fulfillment of his ambition to be a planter. Pork is very good at his job and takes excellent care of Gerald.

Like Mammy and the other black characters in the book, Pork is portrayed in stereotype as a "good, black slave" rather than as a man. Only rarely do Pork's own feelings on any subject become known. The most memorable occasion is during the starvation time at Tara when Pork, like Mammy, refuses to work the fields. His sense of self and his own worth is too wrapped up in the kind of labor he does to permit this.

Pork is married to Dilcey and has a step-daughter, Prissy.

SUELLEN O'HARA

Christened Susan Elinor, but always called Suellen, Scarlett's younger sister is a character who is seen mostly through the eyes of others. She shares with Scarlett the characteristic of selfishness as can be seen easily in the book when the girls argue about dresses for the Wilkes' barbecue. Suellen has listened carefully to the teachings of Mammy and Ellen and is far less willful with them than is Scarlett. A good example of this occurs on the barbecue day when Suellen willingly eats the huge meal brought by Mammy. Scarlett fights Mammy heartily on this issue.

Suellen has always lived in the shadow of her older sister and resents it. While Scarlett has dozens of beaux, Suellen's only devotee is the "ginger-whiskered" Frank Kennedy who is more than twice her age. And on the day of the barbecue Frank, along with all the other bachelors, flits around Scarlett with Scarlett's express encouragement. Suellen is furious.

Later, after the siege of Atlanta and Scarlett's return to war-stricken Tara, Suellen is totally uncooperative. She seems to grasp the situation but sees it as only temporary, blaming much of their discomfort on Scarlett's meanness rather than on the war itself. And she is either unwilling to do or incapable of doing the sustained labor necessary to keep them alive.

Her engagement to Frank Kennedy and Scarlett's subsequent poaching of him result in a bitter but truthful letter from Suellen to Scarlett which strains an already unhappy relationship from then on. But the worst comes when Suellen's true colors are revealed at the time of Gerald's death. In this **episode**, the author reveals completely that Suellen is every bit as unscrupulous and money-hungry as Scarlett, only less well-equipped to deal with the situation. In trying to get her father to sign the Iron Clad oath to gain Yankee compensation for war losses, she is totally ruthless and she earns the censure of the whole community.

Suellen's ultimate marriage to Will Benteen is socially significant in that it demonstrates how the social stratification system weakens in times of stress.

CARREEN O'HARA

The youngest of the O'Hara girls, Carreen (christened Caroline Irene), is barely out of her childhood at the opening of the novel. In fact, she is allowed to go to the barbecue at Twelve Oaks but she is not permitted to go to the ball planned for that night because she is a year too young.

Carreen appears to be the only O'Hara daughter who lacks a consuming selfishness and money lust. She, too, lives in Scarlett's shadow when it comes to beaux but she is much less bitter than Suellen. Her secret love is Brent Tarleton and as the story begins, Brent is madly in love with Scarlett. After Scarlett's marriage and removal to Atlanta, Brent returns from the war and comes to Tara to court Carreen. They become engaged at Christmas in 1862. But Brent is killed at Gettysburg and life for Carreen is never the same.

After her recovery from typhoid, Carreen is much more willing to work than her sister Suellen but really physically less able to do so. She is sweet and compliant with Scarlett's wishes but she lives in the world of her prayers and meditations. Carreen never understands the gravity of the situation at Tara and is, therefore, of little help to Scarlett. Ultimately, Carreen enters the convent at Charleston.

DILCEY

At the opening of the novel, Gerald is visiting Twelve Oaks to buy Dilcey from John Wilkes. Pork and Dilcey have married and Gerald is buying the wife of his valet to keep him content. In addition, he buys Dilcey's daughter Prissy so that Dilcey will not be unhappy without her at Tara.

Dilcey is a tall dignified black woman. Though not treated at all fully, she may be the most thoroughly examined of the book's black characters. Dilcey is part Indian and much is made of her difference from the others. She is enormously grateful to Gerald not only for buying her but for buying her daughter as well. Later, Dilcey has the opportunity to return the favor. When things are desperate at Tara and there is no one to help harvest, Dilcey alone works side by side with Scarlett, getting in what little cotton is still standing.

PRISSY

Dilcey's daughter makes more of an appearance than either Pork or Dilcey for it is she who accompanies Scarlett and Wade to Atlanta for the visit at Aunt Pitty's. From the beginning, Prissy's ineptitude as a servant is clear. It is a recurrent **theme** and the author uses this feature of her character to move the plot of the novel along. At their arrival in Atlanta, Uncle Peter begins to chide Scarlett about Prissy's care of the infant and the stage is set for later disasters. Prissy's worst moment comes when Melanie's baby is expected. She has told Scarlett not to worry because she knows all about birthing. But when Melly's labor begins in the middle of the siege of Atlanta, Prissy confesses that she knows nothing of midwifery. From this point until they get back to Tara, Prissy tries Scarlett's patience sorely, And Scarlett reacts without a shred of the kindliness that her mother would have shown.

Prissy is an exceedingly stereotyped figure whose major function in the novel is some comic relief and as a minor catalyst to the action.

JONAS WILKERSON

Jonas Wilkerson is dismissed from his job as Tara's Yankee overseer as the book opens. He has fathered Emmy Slattery's illegitimate child and is not welcome to stay on at his post. He is bitter and resentful of those at Tara anyway and this dismissal fills him with hatred. Years later, after the war, when he has gained power with the Yankee occupation government, Wilkerson's hatred comes to full bloom. He sees to it that the taxes are raised on Tara hoping the O'Haras will default so he can buy the place at a sheriff's sale.

As Margaret Mitchell paints him, Jonas Wilkerson is an almost totally evil character, with no visible redeeming characteristics. He despises his employers who have quietly but firmly shut all the social doors to on him. And when the war has changed their fortunes he returns to attack with a vengeance. Rebuffed in his attempt to get Tara, he uses his position in the Freedmen's Bureau to foment trouble among the freed slaves. Ultimately, this costs him his life. Tony Fontaine shoots Jonas, holding him responsible for trouble with the newly free Negroes.

Because he is portrayed as such an evil man, Jonas Wilkerson is one of the more unbelievable characters in a novel filled with generally credible types.

EMMY SLATTERY

Daughter of the "poor white trash" Slatterys who live near Tara, Emmy figures only peripherally in the novel and the reader is never exposed to her personality. Early in the story she gives birth to Jonas Wilkerson's illegitimate child who dies at birth. Later, she gets typhoid which she spreads to Tara and which finally kills Ellen. This would have been enough to earn her the hatred of Scarlett but when, as Mrs. Jonas Wilkerson, she comes to Tara with her husband to try to purchase the plantation, all Scarlett's deepest, most vile reactions come to the fore. While Emmy is never personally portrayed, she is the cause of some important action in the novel.

JOHN WILKES

Ashley's father, the proprietor of Twelve Oaks, John Wilkes is the epitome of Southern gentlemanliness. He is the perfect host and his entertainments are large and famous. Perhaps his only peculiarity is his love for books and music. It is an idiosyncrasy shared by the rest of his family and one of the major reasons that they marry among themselves so often. If this other-worldliness leaves the family members ill-prepared to deal with crises, it is not really John Wilkes' fault. He could not have raised them differently.

Margaret Mitchell uses this character to provide an exceedingly poignant moment in the story. When the fighting nears Atlanta, the "Home Guard", filled with young boys and old men, is finally called out. Scarlett and the others watch and she is stunned to see John Wilkes, who is nearly seventy, ride by on Mrs. Tarleton's favorite mare. It is heartbreaking for Scarlett to realize that he is going, probably to his death, with a son a prisoner of war, and his only grandchild not yet born. Shortly before Beau's birth, Scarlett and Melanie got word of his death.

HONEY WILKES

Honey Wilkes is one of Ashley's two sisters and, at the opening of the novel, she is virtually engaged to Charles Hamilton in what will be another of the Wilkeses' within-the-family marriages. Honey does not know how to handle herself with young men and she struts and bridles in a manner very amusing to Scarlett. But Scarlett is not amused when she overhears Honey gossiping about her at the barbecue. So when Scarlett decides to marry for revenge against Ashley, her choice of Charles Hamilton hurts Honey the more.

After the war Honey marries a gentleman from the West in a match viewed with disdain by her haughty sister, India. Everyone else, however, concedes that he is a good man and feels that Honey did better than might have been expected.

INDIA WILKES

Ashley's other sister is a bitter and cold creature who hates Scarlett passionately. At the opening of the book, India (already on the verge of being an old maid at age twenty), has been thrown over by Stuart Tarleton. Stuart, with a little help from Scarlett, has fallen in love with Scarlett and, for this, India will never forgive her.

During the war Stuart begins again to pay court at Twelve Oaks, but he is killed before he and India can marry. India goes into mourning and never again makes much attempt to "catch a husband."

Living in Atlanta after the war, India sees a good deal of Scarlett and hates her more than ever. She blames Scarlett totally for the deaths and injuries on the night of the Klan raid. India always suspects that there is something between Scarlett and Ashley but she can never prove it. When she finds them in an embrace at the sawmill on the day of the birthday party, India cannot wait to rush to Melanie with the news. This causes a feud that does not end until Melanie's death because Melanie takes Scarlett's part and casts India out of her life.

The author does not make a full character of India but provides only a partial portrait. It is enough, however, for her purpose which is to serve as a catalyst to some of the important action in the novel.

THE TARLETON FAMILY

Neighbors of the O'Haras in the County, the Tarletons add color and life to the story. The family consists of the mother Beatrice, an extraordinary horsewoman, James Tarleton, who plays no real role, and the eight Tarleton children. There are four red-haired girls: Hetty, Camilla, Randa and Betsy and four sons: Tom, Boyd, and the twins Stuart and Brent. The latter two are beaux of Scarlett's although later Stuart becomes engaged to India Wilkes and Brent to Carreen O'Hara. All four of the Tarleton sons are killed in the Civil War.

THE FONTAINE FAMILY

The Fontaines are a large County family of the O'Haras' acquaintance. At the head of the clan is Grandma Fontaine who is married to old Dr. Fontaine. Next is Young Miss, in her fifties and married to young Dr. Fontaine, who dies of dysentery at Vicksburg. The children of Young Miss and Young Doctor are Joe, Alex, and Tony. Joe marries Sally Monroe before the war and she bears him a son before he is killed at Gettysburg. Alex and Tony return from the war alive but Tony flees to Texas, sought for the murder of Jonas Wilkerson. Alex is engaged to Dimity Monroe but later marries his brother's widow, Sally.

THE MONROE FAMILY

The reader gets only a nodding acquaintance with the younger Monroes. Lafayette (Lafe), the son, is killed at Gettysburg, his sister, Sally, marries Joe Fontaine and later his brother Alex. Another sister, Dimity, is at one time engaged to Alex.

THE CALVERT FAMILY

Hugh Calvert, the father of this clan, makes the mistake of marrying his children's Yankee governess when he becomes a widower. She is afraid of Southerners and is never accepted by them. The Calvert children (by the first marriage), are Raiford (Raif), Cade, and Cathleen. Raiford is killed at Gettysburg and Cade returns from the war dying of consumption. Cathleen, having lost her fiance (Lafe Monroe), marries the Yankee overseer, Mr. Hilton, in order to insure Cade some final few months of comfort.

THE SLATTERY FAMILY

The Slatterys are "poor white trash" who live nearby Tara. Their daughter contracts typhoid which spreads to Tara and kills Ellen.

WILL BENTEEN

Half-dead, Will Benteen is a one-legged Confederate soldier deposited at Tara on his way home from the war. When he recovers, this Georgia "Cracker" stays on, taking over much of the burden of responsibility for the plantation. He later marries Suellen O'Hara.

WADE HAMPTON HAMILTON

Scarlett's son by Charles Hamilton, Wade is named for his father's commanding officer as was a custom of the times. As he grows up Wade learns to fear his mother's terrible temper and becomes a quiet, mouse-like child around the house. Scarlett never wanted children and takes little interest in the ones she has.

Only through Melanie does Wade feel true love and affection. She is devoted to her dead brother's child and makes life tolerable and pleasant for him. Scarlett is astounded one day to find Wade yelling and playing boisterously while visiting at Melly's house. He never behaves like that at home. But Melanie really has a way with children and Scarlett has none at all. Being nice to her children is one of the things, like being a great lady, that Scarlett is always putting off to a later time.

ELLA LORENA KENNEDY

Ella Lorena, Scarlett's daughter by Frank, did not cause her mother to settle down and give up the business world as her father had hoped. Ella loses her father when she is an infant and grows up, like Wade, a scared, rabbit child, devoid of spirit and personality. Really, Ella is in a sorrier position than Wade because she has no devoted aunt, like Melly, to fill the gaps in her mother's love.

EUGENIE VICTORIA (BONNIE BLUE) BUTLER

The author paints a much fuller, more colorful picture of Scarlett's third and best-loved child. Bonnie Blue is the apple of her father's eye. She travels with him and he indulges her in every way. She is the most engaging of Scarlett's children with her bright blue eyes and thick, curly, dark hair. Physically, Bonnie most resembles her maternal grandfather. And her personality is more interesting than her siblings' because her mother has not been permitted to break her spirit. For all his spoiling of her, Rhett ensures that she will be a spirited, unafraid child.

In fact, Bonnie is only afraid of one thing - the dark. She has terrifying nightmares from which she awakes screaming. Her mother does not wish her to be indulged, but Rhett insists that a candle be left burning at all times in her room. Finally, she sleeps in Rhett's room as a result of her night terrors. After her death, Mammy admits to Rhett that it was she who frightened her of the dark because she was concerned by Bonnie's wandering about the house alone at night. Rhett forgives Mammy.

When Rhett realizes that Scarlett's other children are being excluded from the social scene in Atlanta, he hurriedly tries to ensure her place. Bonnie's own engaging personality helps him in this as he takes her to Democratic meetings and drives around Atlanta with her. In fact, Rhett's devotion to her daughter helps to win back a place for him in Atlanta society when, otherwise, it might have been lost forever.

Bonnie's untimely death in a fall from her pony drives a further wedge between the parents. A distraught Rhett will not even allow her to be buried until convinced to do so by Melanie. And not until too late is Scarlett able to tell Rhett that she does not blame him for the child's death.

BEAU WILKES

Beau is Ashley and Melanie's son and only child. He is born during the siege of Atlanta and grows to be a loved and loving little boy.

CHARLES HAMILTON

Scarlett's first husband makes but a brief appearance in *Gone With the Wind*. Melanie's brother, he is a sweet, shy boy given to sudden blushes and totally inept as a flirt. At the beginning of the novel he is virtually engaged to Honey Wilkes but, under Scarlett's attentions, he loses his heart to her completely. No one could be more surprised than Charles when Scarlett encourages and accepts his proposal but he does not let surprise deter him.

Charles' untimely death of pneumonia two months after his wedding spared him, do doubt, from a few unpleasant facts about his bride that Frank Kennedy was later to discover.

FRANK KENNEDY

Frank Kennedy, Scarlett's second husband, is a "typed" character who reflects a certain kind of Southern Gentleman and the essence of fussy bachelorhood. The reader first meets Frank early in the novel as Suellen's beau at the barbecue. He is fussy and fortyish, devoted to Suellen, but too shy to propose. He scratches at his reddish beard, fumbles for words and is generally inept. But it is Frank who has brought his business companion Rhett Butler to the Barbecue providing for Scarlett's and Rhett's first meeting, so he serves an important introductory function.

Later, after the war, the reader sees him as a shopkeeper hoping to save enough to marry Suellen. He has, as a Southern gentleman, very definite notions about what a lady is and is capable of, and he applies all these notions to Scarlett with her encouragement. After their marriage he reacts with chivalry when he discovers that Scarlett is far from what his dreams of a wife were. Rather than fight her, however, he gives in because she makes his life so miserable when she doesn't get her own way.

Only in the completely masculine world of the defense of women against the abuses of the freed slaves does Frank lose his nervousness and become quietly determined. When Tony Fontaine comes to the Kennedys for aid in escaping the Yankees, and after Scarlett is attacked near Shantytown, a new, more powerful and distinguished Frank Kennedy emerges. And it is in this guise that he loses his life, in a Klan raid to avenge Scarlett's attack.

SARAH JANE HAMILTON (AUNT PITTYPAT)

Aunt Pittypat Hamilton, so nicknamed by her father in reference to her tiny pattering feet, is another typed character who provides Scarlett with a home in Atlanta. She is the sister of the deceased father of Melanie and Charles Hamilton and has served as surrogate parent to them.

Aunt Pitty is in reality a silly old lady, truly very kind, but full of vaporings and fainting spells. The house on Peachtree Street, where Melanie and Charles have grown up, is a thoroughly feminine one with no boisterous behavior and a good deal of deferring to the opinions of others. The only male influence, besides the deceased Charles, is Aunt Pitty's brother, Uncle Henry, but she is hardly on speaking terms with him.

Throughout the work Aunt Pitty remains a flat character whose very malleability aids the progress of the plot. For example, she is unable to be firm when Scarlett's behavior is unsuitable and, later, she cannot turn Rhett Butler away even when he is not received all over the rest of Atlanta. Aunt Pittypat is a good example of the author's skill in creating a character whose personality flaws enable the plot of the novel to be moved further along.

UNCLE PETER

Uncle Peter is the black majordomo of the Hamilton family. He directs Aunt Pittypat's life and has as rigid a sense of the proprieties as Mammy. From his place in the Kitchen, Uncle Peter makes practically all of the major decisions concerning the upbringing of Melanie and Charles Hamilton and tries to continue to do so with Scarlett after she arrives from Tara with Charles' baby.

Miss Mitchell uses Uncle Peter to help move the action along during the Reconstruction period. Scarlett is driven to and from the sawmill and around Atlanta by Peter until he refuses to do so because she exposes him to Yankees who taunt and embarrass him. His refusal puts Scarlett in the position of driving herself which leads to important events in the storyline.

BELLE WATLING

Belle Watling is another of Margaret Mitchell's typed characters. Here is the prostitute with the heart of gold with even the finishing touch of dyed red hair. She is introduced into the novel when Scarlett first spies her upon Scarlett's arrival in bustling Atlanta. Uncle Peter's careful non-use of "Mrs." or "Miss" in his uninformative explanation of her gives away immediately what she is. Belle runs of flourishing business in wartime Atlanta and, as a loyal Confederate wishes to contribute to the "Glorious Cause." The author aptly demonstrates Belle's negative social standing by having Atlanta's worthy matrons refuse her money - even for the Cause. Only good-hearted Melanie will see that her contribution is delivered.

Throughout the novel a strong relationship between Belle and Rhett Butler is alluded to and hinted at but the reader is never confronted directly with the two of them. No dialogue occurs between them. Scarlett is always curious about and angered by this relationship from the moment she sees that Belle's contribution to the Cause is wrapped in Rhett's handkerchief.

Ultimately it is confirmed that Rhett owns Belle's "sporting house" and, at the end of the story, Rhett does not bother to hide from Scarlett the fact that they live together. Belle's ignorant adoration of Rhett has often substituted for Scarlett's lack of love. It is never confirmed but hinted at that they have a boy child at school in New Orleans. In separate conversations, Rhett tells Scarlett that he has a male ward in New Orleans and Belle tells Melly that she has a son away at school. This is never pursued beyond this point and the reader is free to draw his own conclusions.

All in all Belle is a stock figure whose shining moment comes when she alibis for the men after the Klan raid. It is one of the most comic touches in the book that the author chose to use Belle and her house to exonerate the upstanding cream of Atlanta society. The effects of the **episode** are material for some of the funniest scenes in an otherwise serious work.

THE ELSINGS

Mrs. Elsing is one of Atlanta's pre-war social leaders. Her daughter, Fanny Elsing, loses her fiance, Dallas McLure, at Gettysburg and later marries Tommy Wellburn. Hugh Elsing, Fanny's brother, survives the war but is ill-equipped for the Reconstruction. Scarlett hires him to run one of her mills but he does poorly so she demotes him and moves Ashley in as his superior.

THE MEADES

Dr. Meade is Atlanta's pompous, leading physician and his wife a town social leader. They are quite involved with Scarlett when she lives in Atlanta. The Meades' elder son Darcy is killed at Gettysburg and the younger son Phil dies during the siege of Atlanta.

THE MERRIWETHERS

Mrs. Merriwether is the head of this family and a driving social force in Atlanta. Her daughter, Maybelle, marries a French

Confederate soldier from New Orleans named Rene Picard. During the Reconstruction, Rene and Grandpa Merriwether drive a pie wagon for Mrs. Merriwether who begins a thriving bakery business.

THE MCLURES

The Misses Faith and Hope McLure are two old spinster ladies, neighbors of Miss Pitty in Atlanta. They lose their young brother, Dallas, at Gettysburg.

BIG SAM

The huge black foreman of Tara is taken by the Southern army to help dig trenches. He goes north and then returns to Atlanta where he sees Scarlett and begs help to return to Tara. It is big Sam whom Scarlett awaits on the Shantytown road on the night she is attacked. Big Sam, in fact, saves her from more harm.

ARCHIE

Margaret Mitchell uses the character of Archie to do two things: to move the story along by playing off of his particular idiosyncrasies and to bring another dimension of historical reality to the novel. Archie is an old reprobate whom Melanie allows to sleep in the cellar. After the birth of Ella Lorena, Frank forbids Scarlett to ride around Atlanta alone and has the buggy locked up. Uncle Peter has been slighted and will not drive her. So Melanie offers Archie as a driver, feeling that he is a harmless old soul. Melly feels this way in spite of the fact that she knows he is a wife-killer and an ex-convict.

Archie has spent more than forty years in the Milledgeville jail for the murder of his wife. He obviously considers the crime minor and no more than she deserved for she had been having an affair with Archie's brother. During the war, Archie, along with others, is offered pardon to reinforce the Confederate troops. This he gladly did and now he is free in Atlanta and willing to do odd jobs like driving Scarlett around.

The character of Archie is based on the actual facts of the time as are the convicts that Scarlett leases later on. It is at this point that Archie refuses to drive Scarlett, setting the stage for the attack upon her and the subsequent Klan raid. Archie remains devoted to Melanie but she dismisses him when he reports that he has seen Scarlett and Ashley embracing at the mill. She simply will not take his word above that of her husband and well-loved sister-in-law.

JOHNNIE GALLEGHER

The member of a construction gang in Reconstruction Atlanta, Johnnie is hired by Scarlett to run her sawmill. He is a tough, cruel Irishman and he makes slaves of the leased convicts. It is suspected that he murders one of them.

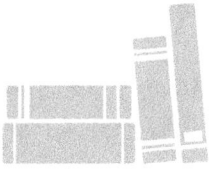

GONE WITH THE WIND

CRITICISM

The aspect of Margaret Mitchell's work that gained greatest favor with the critics was the story itself. *Commonweal's* reviewer called it "storytelling on a grand scale" while in America its "story value" was praised. Henry Steele Commager lavished praise on the "narrative vigor, the sweep and abundance and generosity of incident and of drama."

Not only was Miss Mitchell's story-telling ability remarked upon but also her skill in sustaining the high level of the story throughout the work. The review in the *Manchester Guardian* claimed that the "story never flags," while the *London Times* touted the story's "length which sustained an even level of unquestioned competence." *The Christian Science Monitor's* reviewer claimed that "though *Gone With the Wind* numbers a thousand pages it never falls below pitch." And the *New York Times'* reviewer J. D. Adams called *Gone With the Wind* "a superb piece of storytelling which nobody who finds pleasure in the art of fiction can afford to neglect."

A second feature of the novel which met with critical appreciation was Miss Mitchell's characterization. D. L. Mann, writing in the *Boston Transcript*, felt that *Gone With the Wind* was a "noteworthy achievement" especially in its character treatment and that "Scarlett O'Hara is a heroine to be long remembered." The reviewer for America commented favorably on Miss Mitchell's "restraint" in her handling of "two characters as dramatic and colorful as Scarlett and Rhett," while Commager in his review remarked on her ability to give her characters "animation and reality." Michael Williams, reviewing in *Commonweal*, was ebullient on this aspect of the novel. "It swarms with living human beings, personalities rather than mere characters," he wrote.

While there was little adverse criticism of her characterization, some did appear. An example is Peter Quennell, writing in *New Statesman* and *Nation*, who felt that "her rendering of character seems to owe more to her study of fiction than to her observation of human life."

Another feature of the work which was mentioned often in reviews was its reliance on and use of historical background. Henry Steele Commager and D. L. Mann (writing in the *Boston Transcript*) both comment on its "historical authenticity." W. L. Caswell pointed out that the historical viewpoint is Southern but that the novel captures all the "aspects of that attitude." And *New Republic* concedes an "extraordinary sense of detail" in the historical aspects of *Gone With the Wind*. Perhaps the highest praise of this aspect of the novel came from Jonathan Schnell writing in Forum when he says that it "gives the impression that it was written by one who had really been through the war, was personally affected by the events and battles, but yet had kept some perspective about people and happenings …"

In this context also was some criticism of the Southern bias which is a universal feature of the novel. Largely this was aimed at the novel's uncritical presentation of pre-war Southern life and of the institution of slavery. Noteworthy in this respect was Malcolm Cowley's review in *New Republic* which expressed the feeling that the "legend is false in part and silly in part and vicious in its general effect on Southern life today." Evelyn Scott, writing in the *Nation*, felt that Margaret Mitchell wrote with the "bias of passionate regionalism" and "gives us our Civil War through Southern eyes exclusively."

Among the reviews which expressed a negative opinion of *Gone With the Wind* was that of I.M. Paterson, writing in *Books*. This critic declared that "the writing is redundant and devoid of distinction; Miss Mitchell is apt to make two words grow where even one would be superfluous." In this vein, Jonathan Schnell, who reviewed the book favorably in *Forum*, felt it was "too long".

J. P. Bishop's *New Republic* review criticized *Gone With the Wind* on another count. Here the criticism revolved around Miss Mitchell's handling of the main moral problem of the book: "In a society falling apart, upon what terms can the individual afford to survive?" The ambivalence present in the novel's answer to this question is noted. Scarlett accepts life's terms and parts with all of her old standards of living in order to survive. But Miss Mitchell also suggests, as the review points out, "that civilization consists precisely in an unwillingness to survive on any terms save those of one's own determining." Melanie is, of course, the best exponent of this point of view.

The Times of London, which did praise Miss Mitchell's sustained competence, felt that there was little else to say in the work's favor. And the *New York Time's* review, which generally praised the work, denied it the status of "greatness." "This is not a great novel," wrote J. D. Adams, "not one with any profound reading of life." Both Louis Kronenberger, writing in the *New Yorker*, and Bernard DeVoto were to agree with this assessment.

Gone With the Wind received generally favorable, but definitely mixed reviews. Few reviewers saw it as a great novel with the timelessness of Tolstoy's *War and Peace* but most felt it was a grand story enormously worth reading.

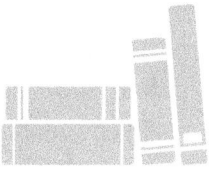

GONE WITH THE WIND

ESSAY QUESTIONS AND ANSWERS

Question: Discuss the major **theme** of the novel and show how the author expresses it.

Answer: The major **theme** of *Gone With the Wind* is that of survival in times of great testing. Miss Mitchell places her characters in the midst of disaster (in Georgia during the Civil War and Reconstruction) and has each work out, or fail to work out, his own survival.

At one point, Miss Mitchell expresses her **theme** by having a character verbalize it directly. She chooses Rhett Butler, a character who survives the disaster magnificently. Rhett and Scarlett are discussing the effects of the war one day and Rhett points out to Scarlett that the war is a time of testing in which the world has been turned upside down. Whenever disaster upends the world, the old order vanishes and everyone is equal for a time. As people struggle to survive, some succeed and soon attain their former high positions. Others fail to make it: They lack the ability, the will, or the treachery to fight other men for high places and so a new order is created.

Mostly, however, Miss Mitchell uses the development of her characters, rather than direct verbalization, to express her **theme**. Rhett and Scarlett are developed as survivors: they attain their stated ends without regard for the feelings or rights of others. Commonplace morality is completely overlooked in their striving after wealth and the security of wealth.

Ashley is clearly not a survivor. Even during the conflict he expressed the idea that war was changing permanently the life he knew and he doubted whether he could adapt to the new life. He fails to do so. Certainly he lacks the treachery, often the will, and sometimes even the ability to cope with the new order of things.

Melanie's survival is more questionable. In Scarlett's terms, she fails. She remains poor and has little hope of seeing her former heights attained. But in terms of her own integrity, she succeeds. She refuses to let the new order of things alter her values or change the way in which she conducts her life. Her early death prevents us from seeing how far this approach could have been carried.

The major **theme** of survival is, then, expressed by both direct verbalization and by the development of the characters. The author makes little comment about the morality of the method of survival - in this the reader is left to his own surmises.

Question: Discuss social stratification among the slaves as exemplified in *Gone With the Wind*.

Answer: The system of slavery in the Old South was characterized by a kind of social stratification that was not dissimilar to that of the white power structure. The first criterion of value was the question of ownership. It was more prestigious to be owned by a large plantation than a small farm (as, indeed, it was more prestigious to own the former). In social contexts, slaves who were the property of large plantations were patronizing to those held by smaller places. An example of this occurs in *Gone With the Wind* when the Tarleton's slave, Jeems, plans on snubbing the slaves of Able Wynder, a small farmer.

Within the large plantation there was a clear-cut social structure headed by the Mammy. The top male slave - usually the valet - followed in authority and prestige. In the case of *Gone With the Wind*, this position is held by Pork.

Other house slaves make up the next rungs on the social ladder - represented in the novel by Dilcey and Prissy - until the outside slaves are reached. It is more prestigious to be a house than a yard slave.

Outside, power and prestige are based on function. All kinds of skills are necessary on a unit as self-sufficient as a plantation and the young male slaves are each given a chance to learn a skill such as carpentry or cobbling. Slaves with these skills occupy higher ranks than those who tend the animals and the lowest of all are the field hands. Slaves are relegated to that position only when they have failed at all else. And field hands are generally looked down upon by those above them in the social system.

Question: Describe the character of Melanie with attention to the question of whether or not her goodness overrides reality.

Answer: Melanie Hamilton Wilkes appears, at first, to be "too good to be true." Having been raised in a household with few tensions and little bitterness, Melanie knows very little of the harsher side of life. She is a happy and good person who has been raised to try to make other people feel happy. Her technique in this is simple: she finds a virtue in the person whose happiness she seeks and she stresses it. Since her own motives are almost always kind and good, she interprets other people's motives in the same light - and, frequently, she misinterprets them. The best example of this is in her relationship to Scarlett. Early in the war, when Scarlett is living on Peachtree Street, Melanie sees in her what she would be in Scarlett's place: a heart-broken and bereaved young widow. When Scarlett cries, Melanie is always sure it is sadness over the loss of Charles rather than anger over the restraints of widowhood.

Only when Melanie feels very strongly about something will she risk hurting feelings to voice it. This occurs at the bazaar when the Home Guard is marching. Melanie declares in disgust that they would all look better "in grey uniforms and in Virginia." Only her deep feelings that it was wrong for the young and able-bodied men to stay at home to "guard the state," could have allowed such a statement in front of relatives of members of the Guard.

In spite of her goodness, Melanie has one "redeeming" fault which permits her to be believable. It is her unforgiving attitude to those who have made themselves her enemies. The reader first sees this point of view when Scarlett murders the Yankee marauder and Melanie, of all people, applauds her action. Her hatred and lack of forgiveness typify a kind of attitude (on both sides), which helped to keep the wounds of the Civil War open and sore. No healing balm of peace can be effective against an attitude like Melanie's. Within the context of the novel such an attitude can be construed as extreme and faithful loyalty but its bad effects are also evident.

This kind of passionate loyalty has an effect upon Melanie's personal life as well. After Scarlett is caught in an embrace with

Ashley which India reports to Melanie, Melanie casts India out of her life. Her blind loyalty to Scarlett causes her to divide the family over this question. Indeed, the entire Old Guard of Atlanta became divided over it. It is, though, a "redeeming" fault. Without it Melanie could not be believed as anything even approaching a real human being.

Question: Discuss *Gone With the Wind* as a novel of social history.

Answer: There are a variety of ways of looking at history and the writer of fiction is free to use any of them. History can be seen from a military point of view or from a political one and both of these types are included tangentially in *Gone With the Wind*. But primarily it is a novel of social history which means that it relies upon the manners and mores of a certain period to provide texture and it, in turn, illuminates and explains those manners and mores.

The social fabric of the South in the Civil War period is displayed brilliantly in *Gone With the Wind*. Miss Mitchell provides her readers with a thorough breakdown of this highly stratified society and examines in detail its highest class. The remainder of the society is seen largely through the eyes of the white upper class.

The kinds of customs and rules which governed the behavior of upper-class people in this society are clearly defined. The definition of a "gentleman" or planter-class male is demonstrated in the descriptions of Gerald and of Ashley Wilkes. The ability to ride, dance, shoot and hunt, the knowledge of horses, the code duello - all were part of being a "gentleman". Acquired culture and knowledge - as demonstrated by Ashley - had little to do with it. And the application of reason, in trying to circumvent some of the more unreasonable customs, could be disastrous.

This is demonstrated by Rhett Butler's negative social standing in Charleston. To Rhett it was unreasonable to ask him to marry a foolish girl with whom he had spent the night walking home after his horse had run off. And it was downright silly to die in a duel with her brother to save the family honor. Refusing to do one or the other, he was ostracized from proper Charleston society.

The rules which defined what a lady was were even more stringent and often sillier. The entire man-woman relationship prior to marriage (and perhaps after) was an artificial one governed by such rules as how long a gentleman must know a lady before he begs to call her by her first name (preceded, of course, by "miss"), and what gifts a lady may properly accept from a gentleman prior to marriage. It was an intricate pattern and Margaret Mitchell exposes it beautifully through Ellen, Mammy, Melanie, and - most often - through Scarlett's misuse of the system.

It is in the rules governing the behavior of widows that Miss Mitchell does a masterful job in exposing the extremes to which artificiality can be carried. Scarlett as a seventeen-year-old widow was expected to dress totally in black and remain in seclusion for several years. Rhett likens this to the Indian custom of suttee only the latter, he feels, is more humane.

Political and military history, while referred to as they affect the characters, are not exposed or exploited in anywhere near the detail of the social history of this period. Thus *Gone With the Wind* is firmly a novel of social history and a very expert one.

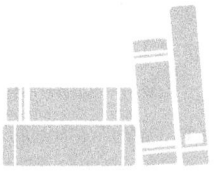

BIBLIOGRAPHY

BOOKS AND PAMPHLETS

Cournos, John. *Famous Modern American Novelists*. New York: Dodd, Mead, and Company, 1952.

Contains a short summary of the salient points of the author's life.

Farr, Finis. *Margaret Mitchell of Atlanta*. New York: William Morrow and Company, 1965.

Long, favorable biography of the author. It is the most definitive piece of writing about the author and contains a wealth of information (obviously prejudiced in her favor).

Macmillan Company Editors. "Gone With the Wind" *and its Author Margaret Mitchell*. New York: The Macmillan Company, 1961.

Handy pamphlet containing some biographical information and telling the story of the publication of the novel.

Mott, Frank Luther, *Golden Multitudes*. New York: Macmillan Company, 1947.

Interesting work which details the history behind various best sellers. Includes several pages on the publication of *Gone With the Wind* and the subsequent furor.

REVIEWS IN PERIODICALS

Adams, J. Donald. *New York Times Book Review*, July 5, 1936.

Benet, Stephen Vincent. *Saturday Review of Literature*, July 4, 1936.

Commager, Henry Steele. *New York Herald Tribune Books*, July 5, 1936.

Cowley, Malcolm. *New Republic*, September 16, 1936.

Quennell, Peter. *New Statesman and Nation*, October 3, 1936.

Scott, Evelyn. *Nation*, July 4, 1936.

Williams, Michael. *Commonweal*, August 28, 1936.

BRIGHT NOTES

THE VIRGINIAN BY OWEN WISTER

Intelligent Education

Nashville, Tennessee

BRIGHT NOTES: The Virginian
www.BrightNotes.com

No part of this publication may be used or reproduced in any manner whatsoever without written permission, except in the case of brief quotations in critical articles and reviews. For permissions, contact Influence Publishers http://www.influencepublishers.com.

ISBN: 978-1-645423-66-9 (Paperback)
ISBN: 978-1-645423-67-6 (eBook)

Published in accordance with the U.S. Copyright Office Orphan Works and Mass Digitization report of the register of copyrights, June 2015.

Originally published by Monarch Press.
Francis R. Gemme, 1966
2019 Edition published by Influence Publishers.

Interior design by Lapiz Digital Services. Cover Design by Thinkpen Designs.

Printed in the United States of America.

Library of Congress Cataloging-in-Publication Data forthcoming.
Names: Intelligent Education
Title: BRIGHT NOTES: The Virginian
Subject: STU004000 STUDY AIDS / Book Notes